The Oxford Percussion Course

(Primary)

Pitch In 1

Jean Maughan

Oxford University Press, Music Department, Walton Street, Oxford OX2 6DP

Pitch In 1

Music making and music reading.

The first stage for Infants and Lower Juniors, of the Oxford Percussion Course for schools.

Teacher's Book
Cassette
Set of 36 Wallcharts

Pitch In 2

Teacher's Book
Cassette
Pupil's Book

First published 1987
Reprinted (with corrections) 1990, 1991

ISBN 0 19 3214458

Typeset by Oxford Publishing Services
Printed in Hong Kong
Designed by Ann Samuel

Acknowledgements

I wish to record my thanks to:

1 Mary B. Wood, (former lecturer in the Department of Education of Young Children, Jordanhill College, Glasgow), for giving so generously of her professional expertise, in helping to prepare the Charts and Teachers' Manual.
2 Walter Blair, (Director of the Junior School of Music, Royal Scottish Academy of Music and Drama), for his splendid assistance in producing the cassette.
3 Alan Stark, (a member of the Scottish National Orchestra), for his help on the technique of playing percussion instruments; Alex Gilfillan, (former Senior lecturer in the Art and Crafts Department of Jordanhill College), for his notes on the making of home-made percussion instruments; Brian Lochrin, (a member of the Audio-Visual Media Department of Jordanhill College) for his photographs of the percussion instruments; Fred Rendell and Steve Bell, (lecturers in the In-Service Department of Jordanhill College), for the words of the 'Pet Shop' song.
4 Freda Hood, for her most efficient and thorough preparation of the typescript.
5 My colleagues in the Music Department of Jordanhill College, for their valued comments, suggestions and support.
6 My father, for his tolerance and understanding.

Foreword

This is indeed a splendid book, and it should prove a boon to
teachers in Primary Schools and, for that matter, to all (specialist
and non-specialist) interested in making music with young people.
It gives me pleasure to recommend it.

This well-produced book contains 36 songs – some familiar and
some less well known. These songs, which are delightfully arranged
with chordal accompaniment for guitar and (or) piano, embrace
helpful and novel suggestions regarding the basic and progressive
use of the percussion instruments normally available in Primary
Schools. The large boldly drawn charts containing the
accompaniments to be learned by the children are in colour; they
will immediately appeal to young children and inspire them to play
convincingly with enjoyment.

Jean Maughan's book with its graduated focus on aural and
reading skills is a valuable addition to current teaching literature.

James Blades

Music acknowledgements

Boosey & Hawkes Music Publishers Ltd (Running, running) Adapted from 'Jumping, jumping' from *Go Ahead* by Dorothy Parr: © copyright 1963 by Boosey & Hawkes Music Publishers Ltd and reprinted by permission.

Norman Buchan (Coulter's Candy)

Essex Music Group (Going to the zoo) Words and music by Tom Paxton. Used by permission of Harmony Music Ltd.

Girl Guides Association of Victoria (Kookaburra) Printed from the Australian Campfire Song Book by permission of the Girl Guides Association of Victoria.

Hodder & Stoughton Ltd (Tommy was a baker) from *Infant Joy* by Dr Desmond MacMahon.

Curtis Brown (Mocking bird and Train is a-comin') Copyright 1948 by Ruth Crawford Seeger. Copyright renewed © 1976 by Michael Seeger. Reprinted by permission.

Oxford University Press (Drive the big bus) melody from 'Roll that brown jug' from *Oxford School Music Books* (Beginners Book 3) by G. Reynolds. (Horsey, horsey) words by C K Offer from *Music Time* arranged by Mabel Wilson.

Every effort has been made to trace and acknowledge copyright owners. If any right has been omitted, the publishers offer their apologies, and will rectify this in subsequent editions following notification.

Contents

Introduction

The aims of this course are threefold:

1 To foster an enthusiasm and love for music, through active participation in music-making.
2 To develop aural and reading skills very gradually, from the playing of simple accompaniments to the songs.
3 To familiarise teachers and children with the technique of playing percussion instruments.

The following skills are introduced in Stage I:

Charts 1–12
Rhythm reading and playing ♩ ♪ 𝄽 on various non-pitched and pitched percussion instruments; time signatures 2, 3, 4 ; bar (box); beats; loud, soft; high, low; fast, slow; long, short; chorus; sounds produced by hitting, shaking, blowing, plucking and scraping.

Charts 13–24
Rhythm reading and playing ♫ ♫ ♩ ♪ ♩. ♪. 𝅝 ;

repeat signs 𝄆 𝄇 ; sharp ♯ ; flat ♭ ; tr 𝆖 ; chords F and C; sound effects; introduction; conducting 2, 3, 4; singing a round in two parts; playing by ear, 3 and 5 note tunes; scale; making up

rhythmic patterns; writing rhythms ♩ ♫ ♩

Charts 25–36
Rhythm reading and playing 𝄻 ; pitch reading and playing, notes B, A G and Low D; stave; G clef or treble clef; bar, bar line, double bar line; correct position for time signatures (also showing 4 as 4);

notes on a line ♩ ♪ ♩ ♪ ; notes in a space ♩ ♪ ♩ ♪ ;

chords G and D; singing a round in four parts; making up longer

rhythmic patterns; writing rhythms ♩ 𝄽 ♫ ♩ ♩. ;

and notes B A G and low D on stave; making up short tunes; phrasing and phrase marks; listening to violin, flute.

Percussion instruments used in Stage 1

Pitched

1 soprano metallophone (diatonic)
1 alto glockenspiel (wide-barred chromatic)
1 alto xylophone (diatonic)
1 set of 20 chime bars, with wooden cabinet
A selection of felt, rubber and wooden beaters
Descant recorder or train whistle (small)
Swanee whistle
Guitar

Orchestral instruments
Violin, flute (or records and pictures of them)

Trolley with flat shelves.

Non-pitched

Skin
10″/25 cm side drum with stand, and a pair of sticks
10″/25 cm tambourine, 10″/25 cm Brazilian tambourine
10″/25 cm tambour

Wood
Claves/rhythm sticks, two tone wood block, a pair of Handcasta castanets, guiro

Metal
Indian bells, sleigh bells, a pair of 12″/30 cm cymbals and a wire brush, 6″/15 cm triangle

Shakers
A small pair of Mexican maracas

Home-made instruments
Rubber drum, flower pot drum, rhythm sticks, coconuts, sand paper blocks, shakers, cardboard or metal thundersheet

Trolley

Before purchasing musical instruments, ensure that they are approved to British Standards whenever possible.

Accompaniments

Guitar

Teachers will soon become aware of the simplicity of the accompaniments, i.e. 3 basic chords, I,
IV and V^7 in the four keys of C F G and D major. These are:

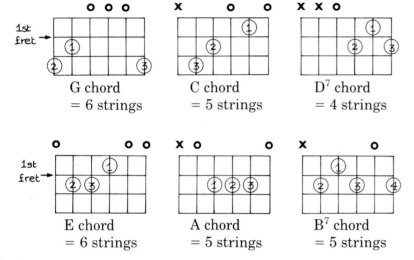

| G chord
= 6 strings | C chord
= 5 strings | D^7 chord
= 4 strings | D chord
= 4 strings | A^7 chord
= 5 strings | F chord
= 4 strings | G^7 chord
= 6 strings |

| E chord
= 6 strings | A chord
= 5 strings | B^7 chord
= 5 strings |

0 = play open string. For chords F, B^b and C^7, play E, A and B^7 with
capo at 1st fret. Alternatively, without capo sing/play melody a
semi-tone lower

× = omit this string.

Piano

As an alternative to the given piano accompaniments, the following
chords could be played at the keyboard, using the guitar symbols,
e.g. in $\frac{2}{4}$ time play in each bar, left, right (i.e. L.R.), in $\frac{3}{4}$ time play
L.R.R, and in $\frac{4}{4}$ time play L.R.L.R. or L.R.R.R.

C major

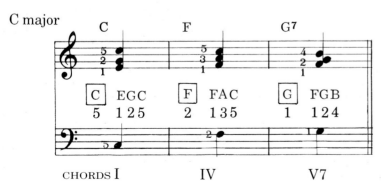

| C | EGC | F | FAC | G | FGB |
| 5 | 125 | 2 | 135 | 1 | 124 |

CHORDS I   IV   V7

F major

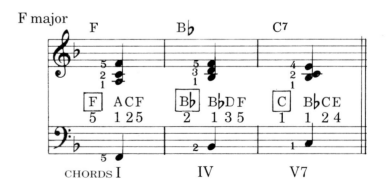

| F | ACF | B$\flat$ | B$\flat$DF | C | B$\flat$CE |
| 5 | 125 | 2 | 135 | 1 | 124 |

CHORDS I   IV   V7

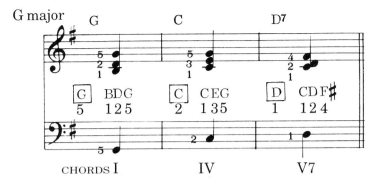

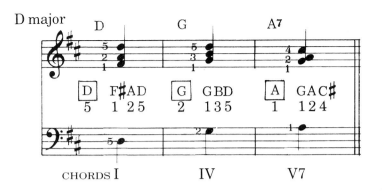

Two teachers might find it helpful to work together, e.g. one playing the guitar/piano while the other organizes the instruments and singing of the children. The cassette should be used preferably at home by teachers who need extra help and guidance. It can also be used for listening and rhythmic activities in the classroom.

Summary of chords: piano and guitar

G major	D major	F (E) major	C major
21, 25, (26)	12		
G D⁷	D A⁷	F C⁷ (E B⁷)	C G⁷
3, 7, 23, 28, 30, 31, 33, 34, 36	2, (23), 19	1, 4, 9, 13, 15 16, 22	11
G C D⁷	D G A⁷	F B♭ C⁷ (E A B⁷)	C F G⁷
6, 29	14, 27, 32, 35	5, 8, 10, 17, 20, 24	18

The melodies of the following 12 songs could be played by beginners on the keyboard:

Song	Notes	Right hand Fingering
26 (*Jingle bells*)	B	3
26 (*Fire engine*)	A B	2 3
28, 3, (36)	G A(A♯) B	1 2(2) 3
23	(F♯) G A B C D D E F♯ G A	(1) 1 2 3 4 5 1 2 3 4 5
27 (chorus)	D E F♯ G A	1 2 3 4 5
30	Low D G A B	1 3 4 5
29	Low D E G A B	1 2 3 4 5
31	Low D G A B C	1 2 3 4 5
13, 22	F G A B♭ C	1 2 3 4 5

The following teaching points should be noted:

1 A rich variety of musical activities should complement this course, e.g. music for (a) centres of interest, (b) specific occasions, such as Hallowe'en, Christmas, etc., and (c) school assemblies.

2 Before starting any formal work with the Charts, young children should have had experience of exploratory and creative music making, as well as the usual pre-reading, pre-number activities, i.e. clapping to speech rhythms, movement to music, and listening games, so that visual and auditory discrimination are well developed, and a start has been made in reading, writing and counting.

3 The teacher must ensure right from the start that the rhythm of the tune can be different from the rhythm of the accompaniment.

4 Instrumental accompaniment should only be added when the singing is of a satisfactory standard. The teacher should always encourage sensitive playing, and listening to the balance of sound.

5 In the initial stages of music reading teachers should introduce the following progression: SOUND; NAME; SYMBOL. Teachers should direct and control the sounds with a tambour.

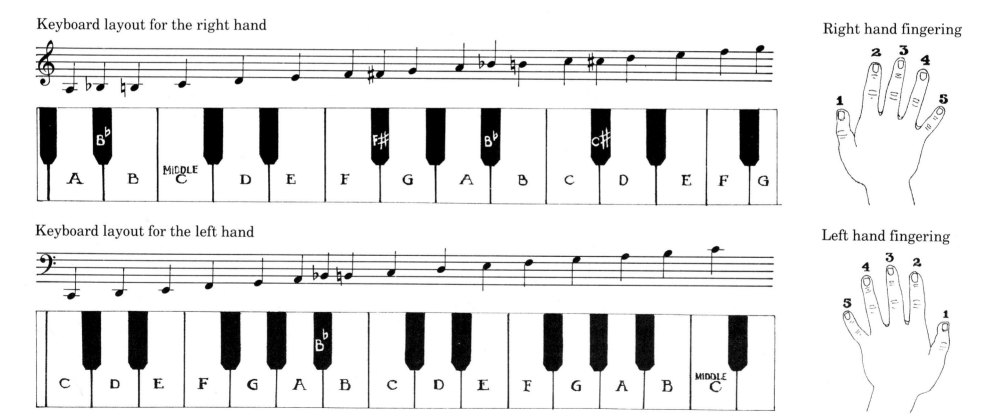

Keyboard layout for the right hand

Right hand fingering

Keyboard layout for the left hand

Left hand fingering

The technique for playing non-pitched percussion instruments

Skin

Tambour
Hold the wooden rim still in the left hand and tap with the finger tips of the right hand at the centre of the skin. If playing loud and soft sounds, try the following technique:

Play the accented notes with the felt head of a beater, and the unaccented notes with the stick of a beater on the rim of the tambour.

Tunable tambours should be tuned diagonally and not in a circle. The hole in the rim, of both the tambour and tambourine, should be used only for storage purposes.

Tambourine
Same hold as for the tambour. Different sounds are produced by different ways of playing the tambourine, e.g. normally use the finger tips of the right hand at the centre. For a softer sound, use only the tip of the middle finger at the centre, or use the finger tips on the rim, so that only the jingles can be heard. For louder sounds, use the knuckles, or palm of the hand, at the centre. Always use a loose wrist movement.

Brazilian tambourine
Hold in the right hand and strike the rim on to the palm of the left hand. By holding it in the right hand, it is also much easier for young children to play a tremolo (i.e. a shake), but this rotary movement of the wrist needs practice.

Drum
If using the traditional primary school drum, make sure that the strap (which goes over the left shoulder and under the right arm) can be adjusted, so that the drum is held at hip height and is sloping away from the body, at an angle of 45°. This enables the beater to make contact, without catching the rim. Use only one beater.

Side drum mounted on a stand
The adjustable snares (a series of wires, which lie across the lower head (i.e.skin)) are responsible for the individual tone of the side drum. When the instrument is not in use, or when practising, release the snares by moving the snare release key at the side of the drum. To obtain different sounds, adjust the screw at the top of this key. For a quiet sound, place a soft household duster on the 'head'. Younger children should use the 'matched grip' when holding the sticks, i.e. they should be held, not too tightly, between the first joints of the index fingers and thumbs, one third of the way up the sticks, and played with flexible wrists. The correct hold for the left hand stick can be taught at a later stage. Play 5cm in from the rim, with the drum in a horizontal position, at hip height. If a drum is not available, use either a tambour or a home-made drum.

Wood

Two tone wood block
A good substitute for claves, and easier to control. Hold it in the left hand, and with the thin end of the beater in the right hand, strike it against one side only, unless two different sounds are needed. Single wood blocks are also commercially available, but if only one instrument is to be bought, the two tone wood block is recommended.

Claves (and rhythm sticks)

The left hand sticks should be supported lightly on the thumb and finger tips so that the cupped hand acts as a resonator. Hold the right hand stick with the 'matched grip', and strike it against the left one. If this technique is too difficult for young children, hold both sticks very lightly with the matched grip, or use the two tone wood block.

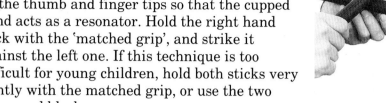

Handcasta castanets

Hold one between the thumb and index and middle fingers. Some children will be able to play two castanets, i.e. one in each hand. The use of authentic Spanish castanets can be taught to older children.

Guiro (or reso-reso)

Place the left thumb and index and middle fingers in the holes underneath, and with the right hand, draw the stick along the top of the instrument. If necessary, the stick can be attached to the guiro with a long piece of string or thin wire. In order to obtain different sounds, experiment with the thick and thin ends of the stick and also a triangle beater, played gently and slowly.

Coconuts

Buy very small coconuts for the young players. Hold them lightly, one in each hand, and keeping the left hand coconut still, move the right hand coconut up and down against the rim of the left one.

Metal

Triangle

There are three parts (a) the triangle, (b) the holder, and (c) the beater. (This is a difficult instrument for young children to control.) The holder is kept in position in the left hand by the second, third and fourth fingers, which are placed as near to the top angle of the triangle, as possible. This enables the first finger and thumb to stop the sound, when necessary. Strike the triangle with the metal end of the beater, on the outer side, near the top. For a softer sound, use the rubber end of the beater. A trill is produced by moving the beater between the two sides of the top angle and lowering it to obtain a crescendo. For holding the triangle, professional players sometimes use a bulldog clip attached to a music stand. This is recommended, as it enables the player to have more control of the instrument.

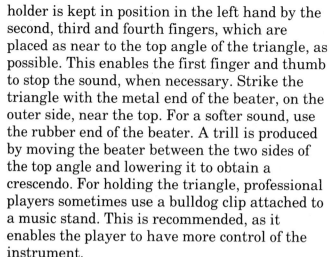

One suspended cymbal

Hold the cymbal in the left hand and with a felt beater in the right hand, strike the beater two inches in from the rim of the cymbal. For different sounds, experiment with a wooden beater or wire brush. To stop the sound, another child could use the thumb, index and middle fingers of the right hand on the cymbal. Alternatively, one child could hold the leather strap while the other child played the cymbal with the right beater and stopped the sound with the left fingers.

Sleigh bells

Hold the wooden handle in the left hand, and with the clenched fist of the right hand, tap the knuckles of the left hand. If this technique is too difficult, hold the sleigh bells in the right hand and play with sharp, short flicks from the wrist.

Indian bells

Young children find it easier to hold the cord between the first finger and thumb of each hand, as near to the disc as possible. Keeping the left hand still, suspend the disc horizontally, and

with the right hand disc held vertically, strike the rim of the left one. Alternatively, try holding the left disc vertically and with the right hand disc held horizontally, strike the rim of the left one, at the top. To stop the sound, either draw them in to the clothes, or use the middle fingers of both hands against the rims of the Indian bells.

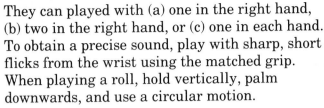

Pair of cymbals

Hold the leather straps firmly with the matched grip, and use a swift up and down movement. For a full sound, turn the cymbals outwards, and for short sounds or to stop the vibrations, draw the cymbals in to the body. Large cymbals are recommended. The following diagrams will help teachers to assemble the leather straps. Before working with the straps, make the leather as pliable as possible, and when pulling the strap ends tight, use a pair of pliers.

Shakers

Maracas

They can played with (a) one in the right hand, (b) two in the right hand, or (c) one in each hand. To obtain a precise sound, play with sharp, short flicks from the wrist using the matched grip. When playing a roll, hold vertically, palm downwards, and use a circular motion.

Turk's knot

1 Spread cymbal straps on inside.

2 Take strap 1 over 2 Take strap 2 over end of 1 and 3.

3 Take strap 3 over end of 2 and 4.

4 Take strap 4 over end of 3 and tuck through loop of 1.

5 Pull strap ends tight. Pliers are helpful at this stage.

The teacher's use of pitched percussion instruments

Basic equipment

Alto glockenspiel (steel bars)
Chromatic model, (one which has bars equivalent to the black and white keys of the keyboard). Use wooden or rubber beaters.

1 box of 20 chime bars in a wooden cabinet (alloy bars)
Indicate by labels (1) the top lid of the wooden cabinet, and (2) the ends of the chime bars, with the appropriate letter names.

A chime bar can either be played on a level surface or held in the left hand. To allow the sound to vibrate, keep the left thumb away from the hole. Use rubber beaters. To obtain a special effect, e.g. a 'wobbly' sound, place the chime bar on a table, strike it with the beater in the left hand, and then with a piece of cardboard in the right hand, draw the cardboard up and down between the sound hole and the metal bar. If an extra bar is needed when playing chords on the chime bars, the soprano metallophone can be used along with them.

Soprano metallophone (alloy bars)
Diatonic model, (one which has bars equivalent to the white keys of the keyboard). 2 F sharp bars and 1 B flat bar are also supplied with the instrument. Use felt or rubber beaters.

Alto xylophone (wooden bars)
Diatonic model made of vibron or rosewood. 2 F sharp bars and 1 B flat bar are also supplied with the instrument. Use felt, rubber or wooden beaters.

Trolley
If instruments are to be shared centrally, the use of a trolley is recommended. Both cupboard and trolley should have labelled places for all the instruments. Timetabling of this equipment may be necessary, if a few teachers wish to use these instruments regularly.

1 Ensure that instruments, e.g. glockenspiel, metallophone, chime bars, xylophone, are laid out correctly for the children, i.e. low sounds (larger bars) to the left of the player.
2 Instruments should be labelled, so that reading the name, e.g. 'alto xylophone' from left to right, also determines the position of low/high notes.
3 Ensure that instruments are placed on a level surface at a comfortable height with the players near the teacher.
4 To help children when playing, the teachers will find it useful to remove unwanted bars. Always use two hands when removing bars, to prevent bending the pins which hold the bars in position.
5 It is important that children are trained to use the correct beaters, i.e. felt, rubber or wooden heads for xylophones, rubber heads for chime bars, rubber or wooden heads for glockenspiels, rubber or felt heads for metallophones.
6 It is equally important that children are trained to use the beaters correctly, i.e. the beater should be held between the thumb and first joint of the index finger, palm downwards, holding the beater about one third up its length, and the wrist should be used in a flexible manner, i.e. the basic 'matched grip'. Children must aim for the middle of the bar and be shown how to stop the sound if necessary, with the middle three fingers of the other hand.
7 When ready and able, the children should play with two beaters, using alternate hands where possible. Although the correct use of left and right hands is indicated in the manual, teachers may have to adapt this technique, and in some cases, suggest one

hand only, particularly when young children are reading and playing at the same time.

8 If there is neither piano nor guitar accompaniment, ensure that children sing in the same key as the pitched percussion instruments, by playing the first or last phrase of the tune on a pitched instrument, before they sing the songs in Charts 1–24.

9 When preparing to play these instruments, children must sing the letter names to the correct pitch, and practise the correct movements 5cm above the bars. Teachers can refer to the picture of the pitched percussion instrument on the Chart, so that the children can see the layout of the bars.

10 If there is difficulty in fitting in the speed of the accompaniment to the speed of the song, tap the beat (or pulse) of the song and transfer the same speed, to the rhythm of the accompaniment.

11 At the start and end of each teaching session, ensure that bars are always replaced in the correct order, and train children to check that this is so. They should be encouraged to be instrumentally tidy.

12 The notes B A G and Low D used in these accompaniments could also be played on a descant recorder, using the following fingering:
(Remember to place the left hand at the top of the recorder with the left thumb covering the back hole.)

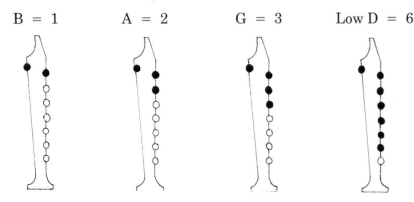

B = 1   A = 2   G = 3   Low D = 6

13 For further details on the use of percussion instruments and the technique of playing them, refer to *Play Tuned Percussion* and *Play Rhythmic Percussion* by James Blades, published by Faber and Co, and *How to Play Drums* by James Blades and J. Dean, published by I.M.P.

Home-made instruments

Skin

Flower pot
Use earthenware pot. Cut two circles of greaseproof or *thin* brown paper two or three inches larger than diameter of pot. Cut circle of muslin or cheesecloth to same size. Use thin cold water paste or cellulose paste. Lay circle of paper on scrap paper or plastic. Paste well. On top of this, lay muslin and again paste, rubbing this well in. Place other paper circle on top, to complete 'sandwich'. Rub from centre outwards to remove air bubbles and most wrinkles. Allow to become supple. Place on flower pot and press paper down over rim. Tie with string. Skin will tighten as it dries. This can be varnished when dry.

Rubber drums
Larger tins, if opened at both ends, make more lasting drums. Collect an old *rubber* inner tube from a garage. Cut two circles 5cm larger in diameter than the tin, from the tube. Do not worry if the rubber does not lie flat. Pierce holes around the rubber circles using a suitable number – even, not odd number. These should be about 1 cm from the edge, and about 2.5cm apart. Thread a strong twine through these holes. Place rubber circles over tin and pull this line tight and tie firmly. Use blind cord to complete the lacing. Working round the drum pull the cord fairly tight. Work round once again, pulling tighter. Gradually increase the tension and test until the drum responds to tapping with a stick.

Claves or rhythm sticks
Cut two lengths of 2 or 3 cm wooden dowel, or broom handle – 20 to 25 cm long. Sandpaper then varnish the dowel. Try different woods; different lengths.

Sandpaper blocks
Use scrap wooden blocks approximately 10×5 cm or date box lids. Glue sandpaper or emery paper to one side of the block. Glue cotton reel on other side to use as handle. Try different grades of sandpaper.

Coconut
Saw coconut cleanly in halves – remove flesh. Rub on coarse sandpaper or file smooth.

Shakers
Use hard plastic containers, (e.g. yoghurt). Place some small seeds, lentils or barley, in one of the cartons. Thinly coat rim of this and another carton with an *impact* adhesive, such as Evo-stick. *Wait 15 minutes*, then place together for immediate bond.

30 Teacher-made workcards

It is important that children should be given the chance to work individually, at their own pace, with these rhythm, pitch and creative workcards, i.e. 15 Rhythm cards, (R.1–15), 12 Pitch cards, (P.1–12), and 3 Creative cards (C.1–3). Teachers may wish to make up further patterns of their own.

Rhythm workcards (R.1–15)

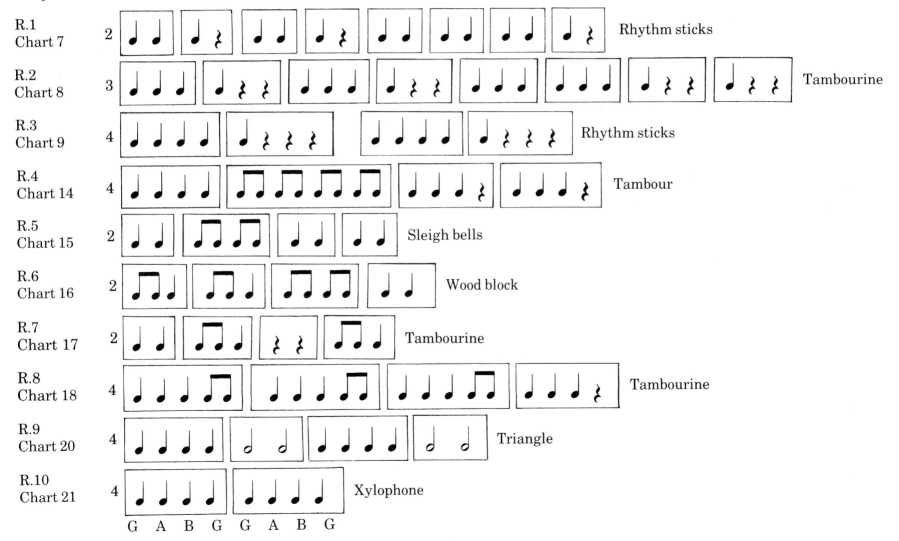

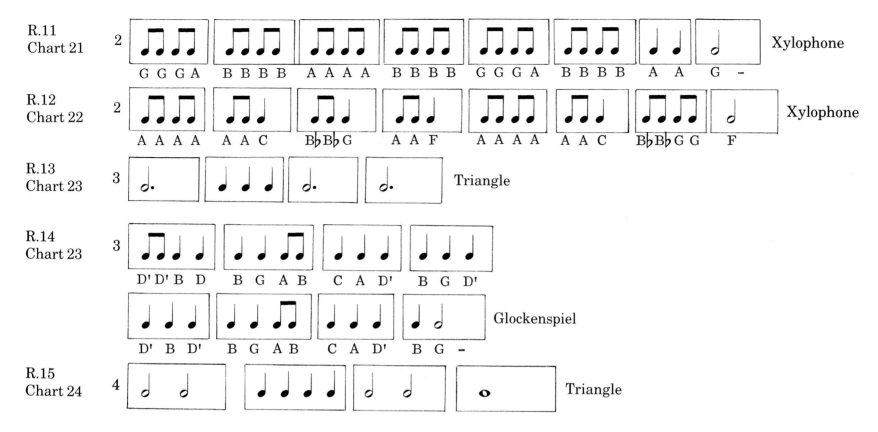

R.11
Chart 21

G G G A   B B B B   A A A A   B B B B   G G G A   B B B B   A A   G –   Xylophone

R.12
Chart 22

A A A A   A A C   B♭B♭ G   A A F   A A A A   A A C   B♭B♭G G   F   Xylophone

R.13
Chart 23

Triangle

R.14
Chart 23

D' D' B D   B G A B   C A D'   B G D'

D' B D'   B G A B   C A D'   B G –   Glockenspiel

R.15
Chart 24

Triangle

Pitch workcards (P.1–12)

Use wide spaced manuscript paper.

Glockenspiel or xylophone

P.1
Chart 26

P.2
Chart 27

P.3
Chart 28

I hear thunder

18

P.4
Chart 28

Three blind mice

P.5
Chart 29

P.6
Chart 30

Come to the cookhouse door

P.7
Chart 30

P.8
Chart 31

P.9
Chart 31

P.10
Chart 32

P.11
Chart 34

P.12
Chart 36

19

Creative workcards (C.1–3)

Glockenspiel or xylophone

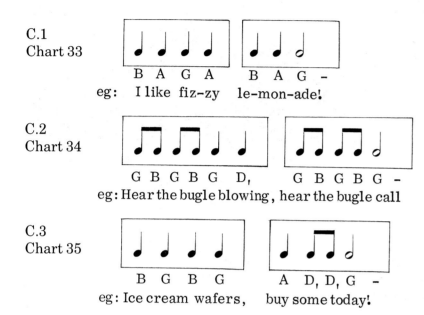

C.1
Chart 33

B A G A   B A G -

eg: I like fiz-zy le-mon-ade!

C.2
Chart 34

G B G B G D,   G B G B G -

eg: Hear the bugle blowing, hear the bugle call

C.3
Chart 35

B G B G   A D, D, G -

eg: Ice cream wafers,   buy some today!

SONGS

1 Walk, walk round the room

American tune

Handwritten: Ring Ring, Ring the Bells, Ring the Bells togetha
Play Play Play the Drum Play the Drum togetha

Introduction

F   C7   F

Count in, 1, 2. 1 Walk, walk, round the room, Round the room to-

C7   F   C7   F

ge — ther, Walk, walk, round the room, Round the room to - ge — ther.

2 Left, right, stamp your feet,
Stamp your feet together,
Left, right, stamp your feet,
Stamp your feet together.

3 One, two, clap the beat, (clap; knees)
Clap the beat together,
One, two, clap the beat,
Clap the beat together.
(See follow up game six.)

4 Play, play, on the drum, *On the sticks*
On the drum together,
Play, play, on the drum,
On the drum together.

Handwritten: Tap Tap Tap the sticks

Handwritten: Ching Ching Tambourine
Tambourine Togethe

(Singers join in with the actions.)

5 Repeat V.1.
(Children clap the 'walk' beat as they sing
and walk round the room.)

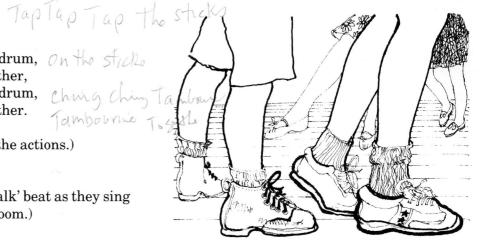

Handwritten: Clap clap clap your hands

22

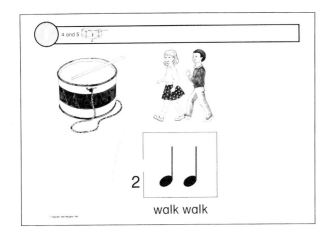

walk walk

Equipment

Chart 1

Guitar chords: F and C^7 (or E and B^7 with capo at 1st fret)
V.4 and v.5 drum with snares: felt, rubber and wooden beaters. Equipment for follow up games is shown in brackets.

To introduce

1 The one-beat note by walking, stamping, clapping (cláp, knées) and playing the drum.
2 The term 'walk' for the sound of a one-beat note.
3 The symbol ♩ for a one-beat note, referred to as a filled-in note.
4 The time signature **2** for 2 walk beats.
5 The bar (i.e. one box = one bar).
6 The drum. Sounds produced by hitting.
7 Felt, rubber and wooden beaters.

Introductory game

'How many different sounds can you make on the drum?' Try various beaters and also your finger tips.

Follow up games

1 Make up other verses e.g. nod, nod, nod your head; sing, sing, sing a song.
2 Teacher or pupil plays 'walk' beats on the drum, while the children walk round the room. When the drum stops, the children stop.
3 'Count the walk beats'. Children close eyes while teacher plays the drum.
4 Teach the singing game, 'The Grand Old Duke of York'. Clap the 'walk' beat for the accompaniment.
5 Tap the 'walk' beat quietly, with Song 1 on the cassette.
6 V.3. Try also with partner, i.e. Beat 1, clap partner's hands. Beat 2, clap own hands.

[handwritten: pat-a-cake on the Beat]

[handwritten notes in left margin: Walk, Skip, Run, Crawl, Bend, Stamp, Hop, gallop, Tip toe, Snap, play, Tap]

Introduction

Count in, 1, 2. 1 What can you play in the band to-day? Band to-day,

band to-day? What can you play in the band to-day? In the band to-day?

2 We can play on the tambourine, ✓
Tambourine, tambourine,
We can play on the tambourine,
In the band today.

Sleigh Bells

castanets,

3 We can play on the Indian bells . . .

4 We can play on the rhythm sticks . . . ✓

5 We can play on one chime bar (A) . . .

6 We can play in the band today
(all the instruments together) . . .

Jessica Drum
Lucy = Cowbell
Varginia = Castanets
AnnMarie = Tambourine
Lauren = Δ triangle

Little Drum

Ringing Chimes

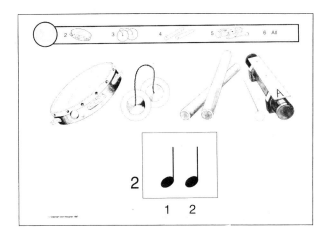

Equipment

Chart 2

Guitar chords: D and A^7
V.2 tambourine; v.3 Indian bells; v.4 rhythm sticks/claves; v.5 chime bar (A); v.6 all instruments

To introduce

1 The idea of counting and clapping 2 'walk' beats in each bar. (Hold one hand still, and tap gently with the index finger of other hand.)
2 The tambourine, Indian bells, and rhythm sticks/claves.
3 A pitched percussion instrument – the A chime bar.

Introductory games

1 'How many different sounds can you make on the tambourine?' Try using your finger tips, knuckles and palm of the hand, at the centre of the tambourine. Try also finger tips on the rim.
2 Can you think of another way of playing the chime bar to produce a wobbly sound?
3 Which is the best way to hold the rhythm sticks/claves, in order to get a clear sound?

To revise

1 Playing one-beat notes on various instruments.
2 Sounds produced by hitting.

Follow up games

1 'Which instrument do you hear?' Children close eyes while teacher or pupil plays instrument already introduced.
2 Mime playing the instruments with Song 2 on the cassette.

Peter hammers

English traditional

Introduction

2 Two hammers (2 hands) . . .

3 Three hammers (2 hands, head) . . .

(Actions: Keep the beat.)

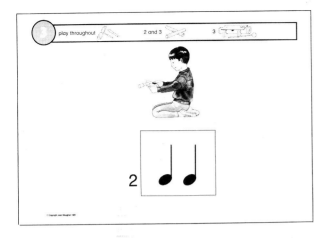

Equipment

Chart 3

Guitar chords: G and D^7
V.1–3 wood block; v.2 and 3 rhythm sticks/claves; v.3 chime bar high D

To introduce

1 The notation for one-beat notes without the visual help of words or numbers.
2 The wood block.

To revise

Playing one-beat notes on various instruments.

Follow up games

1 Make up other verses.
2 'How old is Peter?' Children close eyes while teacher or pupil plays one-beat (walk) notes on the wood block – one for each year.
3 'How old is his big/small sister?'
4 Do the actions, or mime playing the instruments with Song 3 on the cassette.

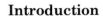

4 A Dutch boy

German tune

Introduction

Count in, 1, 2, 3. 1 I'm a lit–tle Dutch boy, a Dutch boy, a Dutch boy,

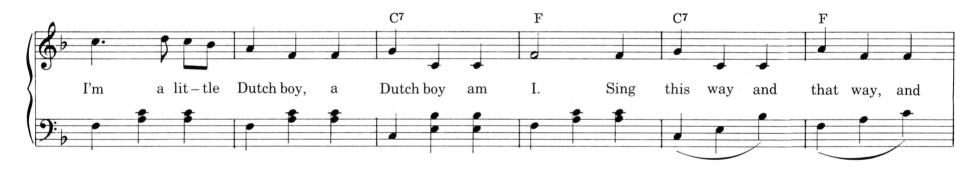

I'm a lit–tle Dutch boy, a Dutch boy am I. Sing this way and that way, and

this way and that way, I'm a lit–tle Dutch boy, a Dutch boy am I.

2 I'm a little Dutch girl . . .

3 We all come from Holland . . .
   from Holland we come.

(Actions: Bars 9–12, Clap 3 beats,
               1   2   3
i.e. clap; knees; knees.
See follow up game four)

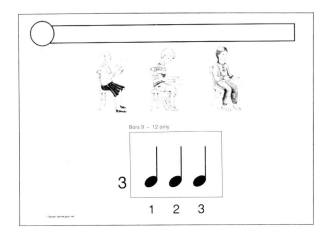

Bars 9 – 12 only

3 ♩ ♩ ♩

1   2   3

Did you Ever See a Lassie
A Lassie A Lassie
Did you Ever See a
Lassie go this way + that

Equipment

Chart 4

Guitar chords: F and C^7 (or E and B^7 with capo at 1st fret)
(Tambour: felt, rubber and wooden beaters)

To introduce

1 The idea of counting 3 'walk' beats in each bar. (Clap¹, knees², knees³) (Bars 9–12)
2 The time signature **3** for 3 'walk' beats.
3 The tambour.

Introductory game

'How many different sounds can you make on the tambour?' Try using your finger tips, knuckles, palm of the hand and various beaters.

To revise

Clapping one-beat notes.

Follow up Games:

1 'Where do I stop?' Teacher or pupil plays one-beat notes on the tambour, accenting the first beat of the bar. Children follow symbols on chart.
2 Bar 8 beat 3 and bars 9–12. As a variation, sing the words 'Clap 1 2 3, 1 2 3' etc.
3 'How old is he/she?' Teacher or pupil play one-beat notes on the tambour.
4 Bars 9–16. Try also with partner, i.e. Beat 1, clap partner's hands. Beats 2 and 3, clap own hands.

(KE Plays The Banjo)

Introduction

Count in, 1, 2, 3, 4. 1 Bob-by plays the ban-jo, the ban–jo, the ban–jo, Bob-by plays the ban-jo, a –

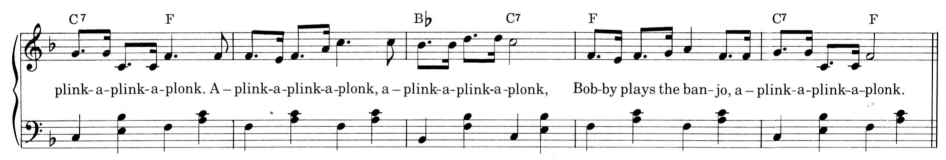

plink-a-plink-a-plonk. A – plink-a-plink-a-plonk, a – plink-a-plink-a-plonk, Bob-by plays the ban-jo, a – plink-a-plink-a-plonk.

(Actions: Children pretend to play a banjo and keep the beat.)

2 Johnny plays the big drum, a – rumpty – tumpty – tum . . .

3 Mary plays the sleigh bells, a – ting – a – ling – a – ling . . .

4 Willy plays the wood block, a – tap – a – tap – a – tap . . .

5 We all play together, a jolly little band . . .

Equipment

Chart 5

Guitar chords: F B^b and C^7 (or E A and B^7 with capo at 1st fret)
V.2 drum; v.3 sleigh bells; v.4 wood block; v.5 all instruments
(Tambour)

To introduce

1 The idea of counting 4 'walk' beats in each bar.
2 The time signature 4 for 4 'walk' beats.
3 The idea of loud and soft sounds. Which instrument makes loud/soft sound?
4 The sleigh bells. Sounds produced by shaking.

Introductory game

Partly fill 8 identical non-transparent shakers with the following: (1) rice, (2) sand, (3) no materials, (4) one pin, (5) dried peas, (6) one pebble, (7) coins, (8) small stones. Which shaker makes loud/soft sound? What is inside it?

Follow up games

1 Make up other verses about other instruments, e.g. trumpet; piano; violin, etc.
2 'When does it change?' Children tiptoe round the room while teacher plays soft sounds on the tambour. When the children hear loud sounds, they stand still and beat the air, or stamp their feet.
3 As a variation, teacher plays loud sounds, followed by soft sounds. Children respond.
4 'Where do I stop?' As before, accenting the first beat.
5 Children sing through one verse, and at the same time, fit in the pattern (clap knees knees, knees).
6 Try also clapping hands with partner, as before.
7 'Which instrument do you hear?'
8 Mime playing the instruments with Song 5 on the cassette.

Yankee Doodle

Nursery rhyme

Introduction

2   Marching in and marching out,
    And marching round the town O,
    Here there comes a regiment
    With Captain Thomas Brown O.

3   Yankee Doodle is a tune
    That comes in mighty handy,
    The enemy all runs away
    At Yankee Doodle dandy.

Chorus

Chorus

(Add actions to the verses.)

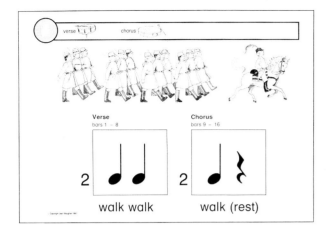

Equipment

Chart 6

Guitar chords: G C D⁷
Verse drum with snares
Chorus tambour

To introduce

1 The pattern which uses a one-beat rest in **2** time.
2 The term 'rest'.
3 The symbol for a one-beat rest.

4 Clapping and playing $\boxed{}$ (Indicate rest by moving hand out to side.)

5 The term 'chorus' (bars 9–16).

Follow up games

1 'Which pattern do you hear?' Teacher claps either the pattern for bars 1–8 or 9–16, whilst children look at the chart.
2 'When do I change the pattern?' Teacher claps the pattern for bars 1–8, then changes to the pattern for bars 9–16. Children indicate when the change occurs. Repeat the game whilst children close their eyes.
3 Mime playing the instruments with Song 6 on the cassette.

1 Drive that big bus

Introduction

Count in, 1, 2.

1 Drive that big bus down to town, Drive that big bus down to town, Drive that big bus down to town, So ear—ly in the morn — ing.

2 Drive that little bike . . .

3 Drive that lorry . . .

(Add actions to the verses.)

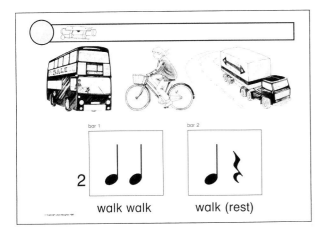

bar 1   bar 2

2   walk walk   walk (rest)

The chime bar should be placed on a level surface. Play the chime bar with the right hand and stop the sound with the middle three fingers of the left hand.

Equipment

Chart 7

Guitar chords: G and D^7
Play throughout low D chime bar (conductor's bell – try firstly on tambourine)
(Guitar, Indian bells, rhythm sticks/claves, wood block)

To introduce

1 A two-bar pattern, as an introduction or accompaniment.
2 Playing a pattern which uses a one-beat rest on a pitched percussion instrument.
3 The stopping of the sound for a one-beat rest by placing the middle three fingers on the chime bar.
4 Long/short sounds.
5 The guitar. Sounds produced by plucking.
6 Teacher made workcard R.1.

Introductory game

Remove the lid from an empty box and wrap a few elastic bands of varying thickness around the container. Discuss how sounds can be made from these elastic bands. Do they all make the same sound? Is the sound the same or different, when the band is tightened?

Follow up games

1 Make up other verses, e.g. drive that big van; drive that 'mini'.
2 'Where do I stop?'
3 Teacher-made workcard R.1, e.g. 8 bars to give individual children further practice in reading the time signature **2**, one-beat notes, and one-beat rests.
4 Children close eyes, while teacher plays a long sound on the Indian bells. When they can no longer hear the sound, they put up their hands.
5 'On which instruments can we play short sounds?' Teacher plays on chime bar, rhythm sticks/claves, guitar, wood block, tambourine.

8 Lavender's blue

Nursery rhyme

Introduction

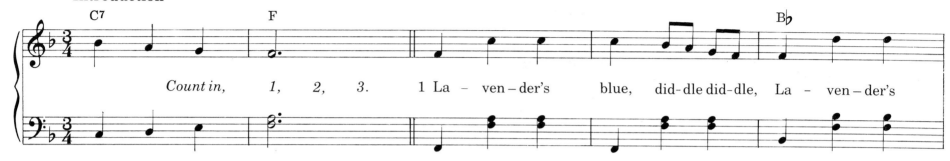

Count in, 1, 2, 3.   1 La – ven – der's   blue, did-dle did-dle, La – ven – der's

green,   When I am   King,   did-dle did-dle, You   shall   be   Queen.

2   Call up your men, diddle diddle,
    Set them to work,
    Some to the plough, diddle diddle,
    Some to the cart.

3   Some to make hay, diddle diddle,
    Some to cut corn,
    While you and I, diddle diddle,
    Keep ourselves warm.

4   Lavender's green, diddle diddle,
    Lavender's blue,
    If you love me, diddle diddle,
    I will love you.

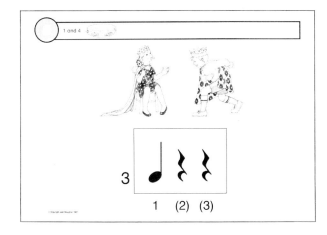

Equipment

Chart 8

Guitar chords: F B$^\flat$ and C^7 (or E A and B^7 with capo at 1st fret)
V.1 and 4 tambourine – play on the rim
(Tambour)

To introduce

1 One-beat rests in **3** time.

2 Playing ⬚ on tambourine.

3 Counting a one-beat rest inwardly.
4 The figure in brackets, which indicates the beat to be counted inwardly.

To revise

1 Clapping and playing one-beat notes and rests.
2 Long and short sounds.

Follow up games

1 Teacher-made workcard R.2, incorporating the time signature **3**, one-beat notes and one-beat rests.
2 'Which words have long/short sounds?'
Teacher says 'Boom! clickety clack, Crash! rat tat tat, Bang! pit a pat, Ring!'
Children think of other examples.
3 Using different parts of the body on beat 1, e.g. hands v.1; knees v.2; etc. tap the rhythm of the accompaniment with Song 8 on the cassette.

9 Tommy was a baker

Introduction

Count in, 1, 2, 3, 4. 1 Tom-my was a ba-ker, Tom-my was a ba-ker, Tom-my was a ba-ker, I

know, I know, I know. All do as I do, All do as I do, All do as I do, I Oh, I Oh, I Oh.

2 Milkman . . .

3 Dustman . . .

(Add actions at the chorus.)

Use this sequence.
Baker fireman
~~Policeman~~
Barber
Farmer
Soldier
Pilot

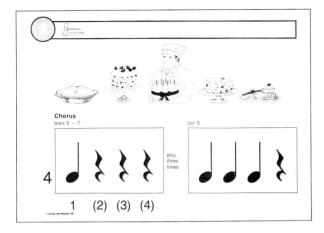

Equipment

Chart 9

Guitar chords: F and C^7 (or E and B^7 with capo at 1st fret)
Chorus wood block
(Tambour)

To introduce

1 One-beat rests in 4 time.
2 A four-bar pattern as an accompaniment.

3 Playing 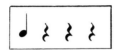 on Wood block for chorus. (Play on words 'All' and 'Oh').

To revise

Clapping and playing one-beat notes and rests.

Follow up games

1 Make up other verses about people who help us, e.g. policeman, doctor, postman, etc.
2 Teacher-made workcard, R.3, incorporating the time signature 4, one-beat notes and one-beat rests.
3 Using a piece of paper, make up more long and short sounds. Try tapping, tearing, shaking, waving and snapping it.
4 'Where do I stop?'

10 Jack in the box

Introduction

Count in, 1, 2, 3. Jack in the Box is a fun – ny wee man, He sits in his box as still as he can, He sits in his box as still as he can, then sud – den – ly up he pops._____

Chorus

Down! Up! Down! Up! Fun – ny wee Jack in the Box._____

_____ Down! Up! Down! Up! Fun – ny wee Jack in the Box._____

40

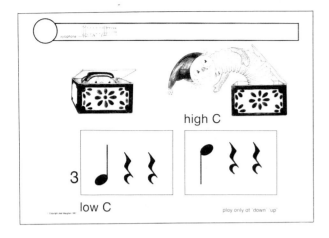

Equipment

Chart 10

Guitar chords F B♭ and C⁷ (or E A and B⁷ with capo at 1st fret)
Chorus –play at 'down', 'up' only, xylophone (low C and high C) with 2 rubber/wooden beaters. Try also playing glissando upwards on word 'up', using all the bars.
(Xylophone with all the bars, Swanee whistle)

To introduce

1 The idea of pitch (high and low sounds), by having the children crouch when they sing 'down' and jump when they sing 'up'.
2 The symbols for high (♪) and low (♩) one-beat notes. (A high note has a 'head'. A low note has a 'foot'.)
3 Playing 2 notes on a pitched percussion instrument for part of the song. (Low C = 'down', high C = 'up'.) Children should be made aware that the large bar produces a low sound and the small bar a high sound. Encourage the use of 2 beaters (one in each hand), as soon as possible after practice of tapping knees with alternate hands.
4 The xylophone (wooden bars).
5 Swanee whistle. Sounds produced by blowing.

Introductory game

'How many different sounds can you make on the xylophone?' Try using felt, rubber and wooden beaters, and also your finger tips.

Follow up games

1 Children lie down. When teacher plays sounds going up on the xylophone, the children rise. When teacher plays sounds going down, they lie down again.
2 After class has sung 'Hickory Dickory Dock', children close eyes while teacher plays sounds going down by step, on the xylophone and asks them 'Is the mouse going up or down the clock?' Children could indicate by showing thumbs up or down.
3 Sing 'Five Little Firemen' from the book *Tommy Thumb* (O.U.P.). This song illustrates 5 sounds going up by step and could be used for further pitch training.
4 'Jack in the box'. Children close eyes. Teacher plays repeated low C's ending with a high C, e.g. 8 low C's, one high C. Children respond with actions to the high note.
5 Teacher removes low C and high C from the xylophone, and then asks a child to come out and replace the bars correctly, by playing them, to check the low and high sounds.
6 A swanee whistle could be used for further pitch training of sounds going up/down.

11 This is how I wash my face

Introduction

Count in, 1, 2. 1 This is how I wash my face, wash my face,

wash my face, This is how I wash my face, ev–ery sin–gle day.

2 Brush my hair . . .

3 Clean my teeth . . .

4 Scrub my nails . . .

5 Jog along . . .

Equipment

Chart 11

Guitar chords: C G^7
Glockenspiel (G and high C) with 2 rubber/wooden beaters
(Glockenspiel with all the bars for further pitch training)
(Drum)

To introduce

1 Playing repeated notes on the glockenspiel using G and high C as an introduction or accompaniment.
2 Singing the letter names of these 2 notes (at the correct pitch) while playing them on the glockenspiel.
3 The glockenspiel (steel bars).

To revise

High and low sounds. Heads and feet.

Follow up games

1 Make up other verses, e.g. 'This is how I play the drum' (they could make up their own drum accompaniment or keep the beat).
2 'Where do I stop?' Children now indicate bar, beat and letter name.
3 Further pitch training, play a few high Cs followed by one G. Children respond to the lower note. For more able children, try with a smaller interval, e.g. high C and high B.
4 Class sings the last two bars of the song, unaccompanied. Then one child plays G on the glockenspiel followed by high C. Class listen and decide whether the last note of the song was G or high C. Play the same matching sound game, with the first note of the song, by singing the first two bars and then playing G and high C again.
5 Do the actions with Song 11 on the cassette.

12 Train is a-comin'

American folk song

Introduction

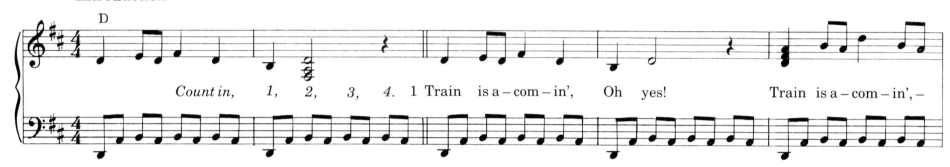

Count in, 1, 2, 3, 4. 1 Train is a–com–in', Oh yes! Train is a–com–in',–

Oh yes! Train is a–com–in', Train is a–com–in', Train is a–com–in', Oh yes!

2 Better get your ticket, Oh yes! . . .

3 Going through the tunnel, Oh yes! (get faster) . . .

4 Stopping for the signal, Oh yes! (get slower) . . .

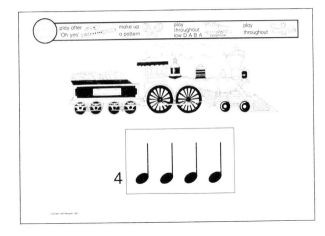

Equipment

Chart 12

Guitar chord: D
V 1–4 train whistle or descant recorder – play after 'oh yes'
V.1–4 xylophone (low D, A and B) with 2 rubber/wooden beaters
V.1–4 sandpaper blocks
V.4 maracas/2 shakers – play a 'roll' on the last note (Tambour)

To introduce

1 Playing fast and slow sounds. Indicate speed by tapping alternate knees.
2 Train whistle or descant recorder. Blow gently after 'oh yes'. Fingering is unnecessary at this stage.
3 Sand paper blocks. Sounds produced by scraping.
4 The maracas.
5 Playing three notes, low D A and B, on the xylophone throughout the verses using 2 beaters. Play low. D with the left hand, and A, B with the right hand, i.e.

D A B A

Introductory game

'How many different sounds can you make with the maracas?' Try long and short sounds.

To revise

1 Singing the letter names while playing them.   2 Sounds produced by blowing.
3 Sounds produced by shaking.

Follow up games

1 Make up another accompaniment for maracas using fast sounds; e.g. play the word pattern from v.2 ('Better get your . . .')
2 'Counting 1–20, – fast and slow.' Teacher starts by counting and playing 1–20 on tambour, to establish a fast speed. Then children close eyes while teacher counts aloud, e.g. 1–8, and children, by themselves, continue counting silently and *tapping quietly* at same speed set by teacher. Children respond with actions when they reach 20. Finally, counting only. Children close eyes while teacher counts, e.g. 1–8 and children by themselves continue silent counting at the same speed set by the teacher. Respond at 20. Repeat game at slow speed.
3 'Where do I stop?' Children indicate beat and letter name, as xylophone is played.
4 Sing the song 'Looby Loo' twice, with the actions. The second time should be much faster than the first!
5 Mime playing the instruments with Song 12 on the cassette.

13 Running, running

Introduction

Count in,   1   and   2   and. 1 Run – ning, run – ning,   ev-ery-bo-dy run – ning,   Run – ning, run – ning,

round the room.   Run – ning, run – ning,   ev-ery-bo-dy run – ning,   Run – ning, run – ning,   all   stop   now!

2   Tapping . . . all join in,
    Tapping . . . all stop now!
    (Practise with one finger in each hand, before
    transferring pattern to rhythm sticks.)

3   Playing . . . all join in, Playing . . . all stop now!
    (Practise with alternate hands on knees, before
    transferring pattern to xylophone.)

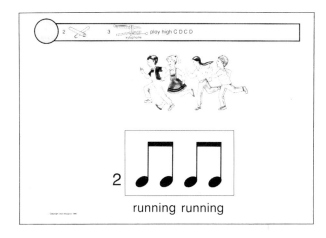

running running

Equipment

Chart 13

Guitar chords: F and C^7 (or E and B^7 with capo at 1st fret)
V.2 rhythm sticks/claves
V.3 xylophone (high C, high D) with 2 rubber beaters
(Tambour)

To introduce

1 The half-beat notes, by running, finger tapping and playing on the rhythm sticks/claves, and xylophone.

Play L R L R

2 The term 'running' for the sound of 2 half-beat notes.

3 The symbols ♫ for 2 half-beat notes. (Encourage children to look for joining bridge.)

Follow up games

1 Teacher plays 'running' sounds of the tambour, while children run round the room, or on the spot. When the tambour changes to 'walk' sounds, the children change to walking.
2 As a variation the teacher plays one-beat notes followed by half-beat notes.
3 'When does it change?' Children close eyes, while teacher plays, e.g. 8 one-beat notes on the tambour followed by a succession of half-beat notes. Children respond to the change in sound. Encourage children to tell how the sound has changed, i.e. from walk sounds to running sounds.
4 'Fun with word rhythms'. Clap your name, clap your friend's name, e.g. Mary Brown = running walk. John Smith = walk, walk. 'Whose name is this?' Teacher plays 'Mary Brown' or 'John Smith' on tambour. Children match sounds to names.
5 Mime playing the instruments with Song 13 on the cassette.

14 Mister Noah

Introduction

Count in, 1, 2, 3, 4. 1 Mis – ter No – ah built the ark, the people thought it such a lark.

Mis – ter No – ah plead-ed so, but in – to the ark they would not go. Down came the rain in tor – rents,

Down came the rain in tor – rents, Down came the rain in tor – rents, but on – ly the ark was saved.

2 The animals went in two by two,
The elephant, the bear and the kangaroo,
They were safely stored away,
Until that great and terrible day.

Chorus
Whenever you see a rainbow . . .
You know that God is love.

48

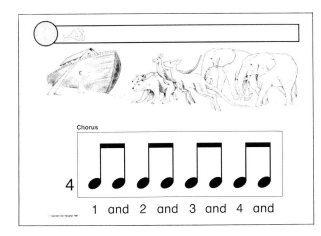

Equipment

Chart 14

Guitar chords: D G and A^7
Chorus i.e. bars 5–8 maracas or 2 shakers
(Tambour)

To introduce

The idea of counting and clapping 8 running half-beat notes in **4** time, i.e.

To revise

Clapping and playing half-beat notes. Remember to use the words 'walk' and 'running' as well as the counting method.

Follow up games

1 'Where do I stop?'
2 Children close eyes and listen, while one pupil walks or runs around the room. After the children have decided whether the pupil was walking or running, the pupil repeats the same movement while the class copy the same sounds by tapping the rhythm quietly.
3 Teacher taps 4 one-beat notes on the left knee, with the left hand, and then follows this by tapping 8 half-beat notes on the right knee, with the right hand. Pupils copy. Try the same exercise, referring to the 'walk' and 'running' sounds.
4 Teacher-made workcard R.4.
5 Chorus. Think of other ways of playing the maracas, to produce the sound of rain.

15 Horsey, Horsey

Introduction

Count in, 1 and 2 and 1 Hor–sey, Hor–sey, don't you stop, Just let your feet go

clip–pe–ty clop, Your tail goes swish and the wheels go round, Gid–dy up we're home–ward bound.

2 Horsey, Horsey, on your way,
   We've made the journey many a day,
   Your tail goes swish, and the wheels go round,
   Giddy up, we're homeward bound.

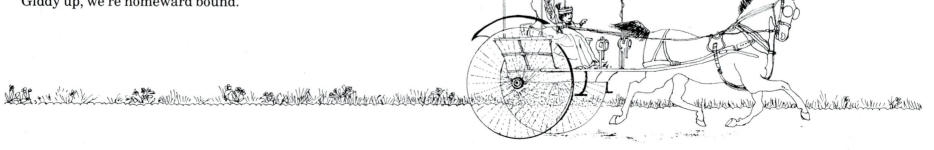

Equipment

Chart 15

Guitar chords: F and C^7 (or E and B^7 with capo at 1st fret)
Play throughout sleigh bells, coconuts and xylophone (low C and high C) with 2 rubber/wooden beaters
Maracas and/or sandpaper blocks – play a roll only at 'swish'
(Tambour)

To introduce

1 The symbols for repeating a part of the music, i.e. repeat signs.
2 The coconuts.

To revise

1 Clapping and playing half-beat notes on the xylophone.
2 Playing a 'roll' on the maracas.

Follow up games

1 Teacher plays running sounds on the coconuts while children 'trot' round the room. When a child plays the walk sounds on the tambour, the rest of the children change to jumping on the spot.
2 'Where do I stop?'
3 Teacher-made workcard, R.5.
4 Mime playing the instruments with Song 15 on the cassette.

16 London Bridge

Nursery rhyme

Introduction

Chorus

Count in,   *1,*   *2.*   Lon – don Bridge   is   fall – ing down,   fall – ing down,

fall – ing down,   Lon – don Bridge   is   fall – ing down,   My   fair   la – dy.

1   Build it up with wood and clay . . .

    Chorus

2   Build it up with iron and steel . . .

    Chorus

3   Build it up with silver and gold . . .

    Chorus

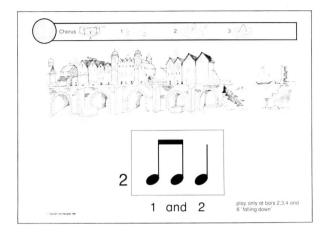

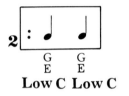

G G   C C
E E   A A
Low C Low C F F

Equipment

Chart 16

Guitar chords: F and C^7 (or E and B^7 with capo at 1st fret)
Chorus drum – play only at 'falling down'
Bars 2, 3, 4 and 6 v.1 wood block; v.2 cymbal with rubber/wooden beater
v.3 Indian bells
6 chime bars arranged in two groups of 3: low C E and G and F A and high C.
This would provide an extra/alternative accompaniment for the Chorus.
(Wire brush)
(Tambour)

To introduce

1 The idea of combining one-beat and half-beat notes in an accompaniment.
2 The idea of children choosing the sound of an instrument which would be suitable for the meaning of the words, e.g. 'silver and gold' = Indian bells.
3 Chords F and C on chime bars, for alternative accompaniment. The teacher must ensure that children understand that sounds of a definite pitch can be played together, and that these combined sounds are called 'chords'. The C chord uses chime bars low C, E and G; the F chord uses chime bars F A and high C. This pattern of chords is played by 6 children, in 2 groups of 3, each child with a chime bar. Place the chime bars on a table so that the left hand finger tips can stop the sounds after each bar.
4 Suspended cymbal with wooden/rubber beater.

Introductory game

'How many different sounds can you make on the cymbal?' Try various beaters, and also a wire brush.

Follow up games

1 'When does it change?' Children close eyes while the chime bar players play e.g. 10 C chords followed by one F chord. Children respond to the change in sound.
2 'Can you tap like me?' Teacher plays rhythm on tambour. Children clap same rhythm. e.g.

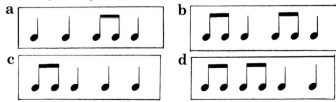

3 Teacher-made workcard, R.6.

53

17 Jimmy crack corn

American traditional

Introduction

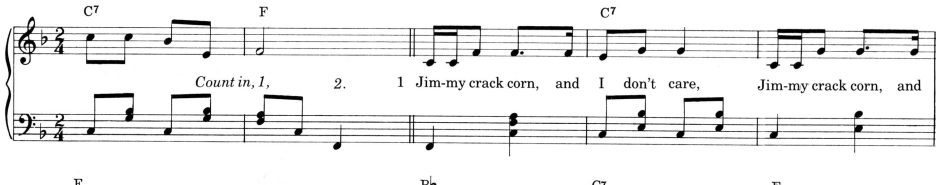

Count in, 1,   2.   1 Jim-my crack corn,   and   I   don't care,   Jim-my crack corn,   and

I   don't care,   Jim-my crack corn,   and   I   don't care, The   Mas-ter's   gone a – way.

2   Left hand out and I don't care . . .

3   Right hand . . .

4   Both hands . . .

(Add actions to verses 2–4.)

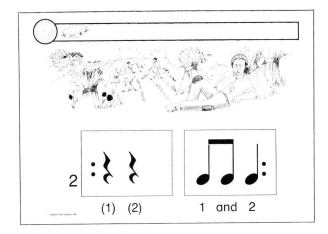

Equipment

Chart 17

Guitar chords: F B$^\flat$ and C^7 (or E A and B^7 with capo at 1st fret)
Tambourine – play at the rim throughout
(Tambour)
(Blackboard)

To introduce

1 The idea of combining one-beat and half-beat notes and one-beat rests in an accompaniment.
2 The idea that in some bars, there are no notes to be played.

3 The idea of children writing one-beat and half-beat notes, e.g. write out Bar 2 for the tambourine.
4 Through further practice of 'Can you tap like me?' patterns, children can be encouraged to convert sounds into word patterns and then into symbols. e.g. Teacher plays a series of

sounds on the tambour.  Children say, 'walk, walk, running, walk'.

Teacher can then write 5 single notes on blackboard and invite

children to chalk in the joining bridges to make the correct one-beat and half-beat symbols for the original sounds.

Follow up games

1 Teacher-made workcard R.7.
2 'Can you tap like me?'

a  b 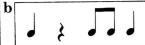 c  d

Teacher indicates rest, by hand movement when playing tambour.
3 'Can you write the music for our song?' Using bar 2 of the tambourine accompaniment, teacher taps out rhythm. Children can then be encouraged to say word patterns 'running walk', and then to write the symbols, i.e.

4 Mime playing the tambourine, with Song 17 on the cassette.

18 The band

(handwritten annotations at top right:) KD   Bass Drum, - Boom / Rhythm Sticks - click / Tambourine   Chink

Introduction

Count in, 1, 2, 3. 1 Oh, we can play on the big bass drum, And this is the mu – sic

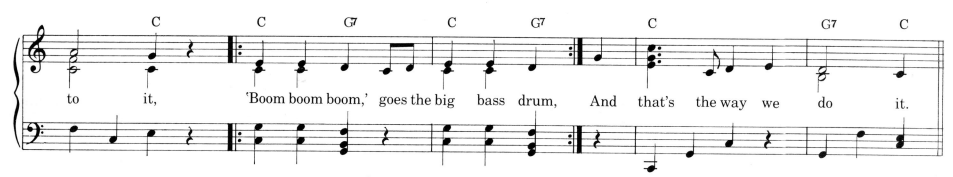

to it, 'Boom boom boom,' goes the big bass drum, And that's the way we do it.

2 Oh, we can play on the castanets,
And this is the music to it,
'Click click click,' go the castanets,
'Boom boom boom,' goes the big bass drum,
And that's the way we do it.

(handwritten:) Do verse 1 – 2 – 3 only.

3 Tambourine ('chink') . . .

4 ~~Indian bells~~ ('ting') . . . *(handwritten:)* Rhythm Sticks –Tap, Tap, Tap, click

5 Xylophone (EED) . . . *(handwritten:)* Ringing Bells

Actions With each verse, imitate the new instrument, followed by
all the others, working backwards to the first one.

56

E E D C D E E D

Play L   L   R   L R   L   L   R xylophone V.5

(3) Bass Drum ~ Boom
3 Castanets ~ Click
3 Tambourine = Chink
3 Rhythm Sticks = Tap.
3 Bong/3X on the Cowbells
3 Triangles.

Equipment

Chart 18

Guitar chords: C F and G^7
Bars 5 and 6, v.1 drum; v.2 castanets; v.3 tambourine; v.4 Indian bells; v.5 xylophone (low C D E) with 2 felt/rubber beaters
(Players should stand together in the correct order)
(Tambour)
(Rhythm sticks/claves and coconuts)

To introduce

1 The idea that children can make up their own rhythmic patterns.
2 The idea of playing two different rhythmic patterns together.
3 The castanets.

Introductory game

'Can you play loud/soft, long/short sounds on the castanets?'

To revise

1 Repeat signs.
2 Which instrument makes loud/soft sound?

Follow up games

1 'Make a pattern for the class/friend.' A child makes up a word pattern and *says*, e.g. 'walk running running walk'. The class/friend repeats the pattern by clapping.
2 'Make up a word pattern in your head'. Child thinks out his pattern, e.g. 'running walk, running walk', then *plays* it on a tambour and chooses a child to repeat the pattern either by clapping or by words.
3 Make up other verses, e.g. coconuts, rhythm sticks/claves.
4 Teacher-made workcard, R.8.
5 'Sounds together'. (a) One child plays 4 one-beat notes on the drum, and at the same time another child plays 8 half-beat notes on the rhythm sticks/claves. Repeat pattern, several times. (b) Teacher taps the walk notes with the left hand on the left knee, and at the same time taps the running notes with the right hand on the right knee. Children copy.

19 Going to the zoo

Words and Music by Tom Paxton

Introduction

Count in, 1, 2, 3, 4. 1 Daddy's taking us to the zoo to – morrow – zoo to – morrow, zoo to – morrow,

Daddy's taking us to the zoo to – morrow We can stay all day. We're going to the zoo, zoo, zoo, How a – bout

you, you, you? You can come too, too, too, We're going to the zoo, zoo, zoo.

2 See the elephant with the long trunk swingin',
Great big ears and long trunk swingin',
Sniffing up peanuts with the long trunk swingin',
We can stay all day.   *Chorus*

3 See all the monkeys scritch, scritch, stratchin',
Jumping all around and scritch, scritch, stratchin',
Hanging by their long tails, scritch, scritch, stratchin',
We can stay all day.   *Chorus*

4 Big black bear all huff, huff a-puffing,
Coat's too heavy, he's huff a-puffin',
Don't get near the huff huff a-puffin',
Or you won't stay all day.   *Chorus*

5 Seals in the pool all honk, honk, honkin'
Catchin' fish, and honk, honk, honkin'
Little seals, honk, honk, honkin'
We can stay all day.   *Chorus*

6 (*slower tempo*)
We stayed all day and I'm gettin'
                              sleepy,
Sittin' in the car and gettin' sleep,
                              sleep, sleepy.
Home already and I'm sleep, sleep,
                              sleepy,
We have stayed all day.   *Chorus*

Equipment

Chart 19

Guitar chords: D and A^7
Chorus (v.1 and 2) triangle
Chorus (v.3 4, 5 and 6) metallophone (low D and E) with 2 felt/rubber beaters
(Chorus wood block-optional extra accompaniment)

To introduce

1 The two-beat note by clapping and playing it on a triangle and a metallophone.

(Chorus v.3–6)
Metallophone
Start playing at 'zoo'

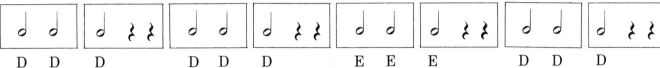

D   D   D   D   D   D   E   E   E   D   D   D

2 The term 'hold (2)' for the sound of a two-beat note.

3 The symbol 𝅗𝅥 for a two-beat note, referred to as an empty note.

4 The clapping of a two-beat note. To feel the second beat and to hold the sound, children must clap hands on beat 1 and hold them together with a slight downwards movement, on beat 2.

5 The triangle.

6 The metallophone (alloy bars).

7 Stopping the sounds by placing the index finger and thumb of the left hand on the triangle.

Introductory game

'How many different sounds can you make on the triangle?' Try playing it with the metal and rubber ends of the beater, also with your finger tips. 'Can you play trills on it?'

Follow up games

1 Add actions at the Chorus, e.g. at 'zoo', (first phrase) point right thumb, left thumb, right thumb over corresponding shoulders. At 'you', point index finger forward. At 'too', cross over hands and tap shoulders. At 'zoo', (last phrase), clap hands.

2 'When does it change?' Children close eyes, while teacher plays, e.g. 4 one-beat notes on the triangle, followed by a succession of two-beat notes. Children respond to change. Encourage the children to tell how the sound has changed.

3 Make up another accompaniment for the Chorus using wood block e.g.

20 Sambalele

Brazilian tune

Introduction

Count in, 1, 2, 3, 4. 1 Oh what a boy Samba-le - le, he ne-ver cares for - work-ing, His days are full of __

plea - sure, from ear - ly morn till __ night, so. **Chorus** Dance and sing and play Sam - ba-le-le, Dance and sing and

play Sam - ba-le - le, Dance and sing and play Sam - ba-le - le, Down at the beach all - day. day. Olé! (spoken)

2 Oh what a boy Sambalele,
   He never cares for working,
   Laughing beneath his sombrero,
   Barefoot and brown, in the sun, so.

Chorus

3 Oh what a boy Sambalele,
   He never cares for working,
   Splashing about in the water,
   He likes to be with his friends, so.

Chorus

Equipment

Chart 20

Guitar chords: F B$^\flat$ C^7 (or E A and B^7 with capo at 1st fret)
Verse tambourine – play rhythm of words
Chorus tambour, rhythm sticks/claves
In the chorus tambour and claves alternate each bar and should face each other
Chorus maracas – optional extra accompaniment
(Triangle)

To introduce

1 The idea of counting and clapping 2 two-beat notes in one bar in **4** time, i.e.

1 (2) 3 (4) Count inwardly beats 2 and 4.

2 The method of illustrating the held beats 2 and 4 is done by linking them with curved lines to the empty notes, numbered 1 and 3.

Follow up games

1 Make up another accompaniment for the chorus, e.g. **4**

using maracas and the rhythm of 'Samba' in bar 1.
2 'Can you tap like me?' Teacher plays a longer rhythm, which includes one or more two-beat notes. Children copy, e.g.

a  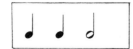   b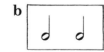

3 'Sounds together'. (a) One child plays 2 two-beat notes on the triangle, and at the same time another child plays 4 one-beat notes on the tambour. Repeat the pattern, several times. (b) Teacher taps the 'walk' notes with the left hand on the left knee, and at the same time taps the two-beat notes with the right hand on the right knee. Children copy.
4 Teacher-made workcard, R.9.

21 I hear thunder

French tune

Introduction

Count in, 1, 2, 3, 4. 1 I hear thun – der, I hear thun – der, Now don't you?

Now don't you? Pit-ter pat -ter rain – drops, Pit-ter pat-ter rain – drops, I'm wet through, So are you.

2 I see blue sky, I see blue sky.
Now don't you? Now don't you?
Hurry up the sunshine, hurry up the sunshine,
I'll soon dry, I'll soon dry.

1 Play the rhythm of the tune on non-pitched instruments.
2 Play the thundersheet introduction.
3 Sing the tune in unison, accompanied by the non-pitched instruments.
4 Sing as a two-part round with glockenspiel accompaniment.

62

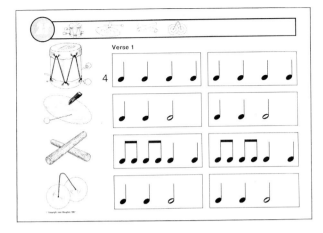

Equipment

Chart 21

Guitar chord: G
V.1 (bars 1 and 2) rubber drum; (bars 3 and 4) suspended cymbal with wooden beater; (bars 5 and 6) rhythm sticks/claves; (bars 7 and 8) Indian bells
V.2 Glockenspiel (G and low D)
(Xylophone (G A B). This would allow children to play the first 2 bars of the tune by ear.)
(Triangle and flower pot drum)

To introduce

1 The idea of singing a 'round' by 2 groups of children. Group 2 starts singing when Group 1 has sung the first two bars of the round.
2 The reading and playing of the rhythm for a whole song.
3 The idea that simple tunes can be played by ear on 3 notes (G A B).*
   (i.e. Bars 1 and 2 of the round. Also the tune *Peter hammers* page 26).
4 The idea of sound effects. Children can experiment with various home-made instruments to provide suitable sound effects for thunder (cardboard or metal sheet) and rain (lentils dropped into cellophone bag). These sounds could be used as an introduction to the singing.
5 Home-made rubber drum, flower pot drum.

Introductory game

'How many different sounds can you produce on the rubber drum and flower pot drum?' Why are the sounds different?

To revise

Playing G and low D on glockenspiel throughout verse 2. i.e.

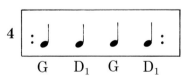

Follow up games

1 'Which pattern am I playing?' Teacher plays bars 1 and 2, or 3 and 4, or 5 and 6 on triangle. Children then match sounds to symbols on chart.
2 'Can you write the music?' Teacher plays, e.g. bars 3 and 4 on triangle. Children can say word pattern (walk walk hold (2)) and write symbols:

   Then try bars 5 and 6.
*3 If necessary, children could be helped with workcards R.10 and R.11 which include the letter names.

63

22 The music man

Introduction

2 Triangle . . .

3 Tambourine . . .

4 Xylophone . . .

(Divide the class into two groups: Group 1 sings and plays the part of the music man in verses 1 and 3, while Group 2 asks the question; Group 2 sings and plays for verses 2 and 4, while Group 1 asks the question.)

Equipment

Chart 22

Guitar chords: F and C^7 (or E and B^7 with capo at 1st fret)
V.1 drum; v.2 triangle; v.3 Brazilian tambourine; v.4 xylophone (F G A B^b C)
(Glockenspiel all notes including Bb and B for further pitch training)
(Tambour)

To introduce

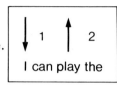

1 The idea of conducting 2 one-beat notes in each bar while singing the verse.(Arm movements when conducting:down on beat 1,up on beat 2) i.e.

2 The symbol *tr* ~~~ and the method of playing a roll on the tambourine and trill on the triangle.

3 The idea that part of the song could be played on the xylophone to accompany the singing. Lines 1 and 3 on chart, verse 4 i.e., 6 As and 1 high C.

4 A further opportunity for children to play individually by ear the whole of verse 4, this time on five notes (F G A B^b C).* Play R . L . R . L . R . L . R . for lines 1 and 3, and L . R . L . L . R . L . for lines 2 and 4.

5 Brazilian tambourine.

Introductory game

'How does the Brazilian tambourine differ from the other tambourine?'

Follow up games

1 'Where do I stop?'

2 'When do I change?' Children close eyes, while teacher plays on glockenspiel a succession of notes, e.g. 8 Bs before changing to a note of higher or lower pitch. Children tell whether the last note went up or down. Teacher can start with well defined intervals and progress to making the children aware of the smallest interval (i.e. the lowering of the pitch from B to B^b) and also the new term and symbol 'flat' (b).

*3 If necessary children could be helped with a workcard R.12 which includes the letter names.

4 Another five-note tune (F G A B^b C) for children to play individually, by ear (i.e. *Running, running,* Song 13). Start on high C, followed by A.

5 Conduct 2 beats in a bar with Song 22 on the cassette.

65

Introduction

Glockenspiel   *Count in,   1,   2,   3.*   'Or-anges and   le – mons,' say the bells of Saint Clem-ents, 'You owe me five

far-things,' say the bells of Saint Mar-tin's.   'When will you pay me?' say the   bells of Old Bai – ley.   'When I grow rich,'   say the

bells of Shore – ditch.   'When will that be?'   say the bells of Step – ney.   'I do not   know,' says the great bell of

Bow.   Here comes a   can – dle to__ light you to   bed,   And here comes a   chop – per to__ chop off your head!

66

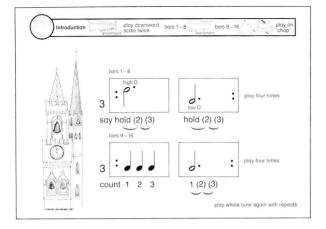

Equipment

Chart 23

Guitar chords: G D^7, D and A^7 (Bars 1–8, 17–32 are in G major, bars 9–16 are in D major)
Introduction glockenspiel (G^1 F♯ E D C B A G) – play downward scale twice for church bells
Bars 1–8 and 17–24 metallophone (high D, low D) Bars 9–16 and 25–32 triangle
A pair of cymbals. Play only in second last bar at 'chop'.
(Glockenspiel – all notes including F♯ and F for further pitch training) (Tambour)

To introduce

1 The three-beat note by clapping and
   playing it on a metallophone.

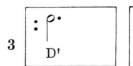 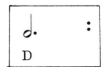

2 The idea of counting and clapping one three-beat note in each bar of **3** time,
   i.e.

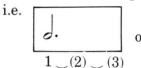

or hold ⌣(2)⌣(3) Count inwardly beats 2 and 3.

3 The symbols ♩. or ♩• for a three-beat note, referred to as an empty note with a dot.

   Observe that a dot, placed after a note, lengthens its duration by half its original value.

4 The idea of conducting three one-beat notes in each bar *down right up*: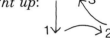
5 The G major scale i.e. G' F♯ E D C B A G. Play R.L.R.L.R.L.R.L.
6 A pair of cymbals.

Follow up games

1 'When do I change?' Children close eyes, while teacher plays on glockenspiel a succession
   of notes, e.g. six F's before changing to a note of higher or lower pitch (as in Song 22).
   Eventually children should be made aware of the smallest interval, i.e. the raising of the
   pitch from F to F♯, and also the new term and symbol 'sharp'.
2 'Can you tap like me?' e.g.

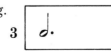 

3 Teacher-made workcard, R.13 and R.14.
4 'Sounds together'. (a) One child plays one three-beat note on the triangle, and at the same
   time another child plays 3 one-beat notes on the tambour. Repeat the pattern several
   times. (b) Teacher taps 'walk' notes with the left hand on the left knee, and at the same
   time taps the three-beat notes with the right hand on the right knee. Children copy.

24 The pet shop

American folk-song tune
Words by Fred Rendell and Steve Bell

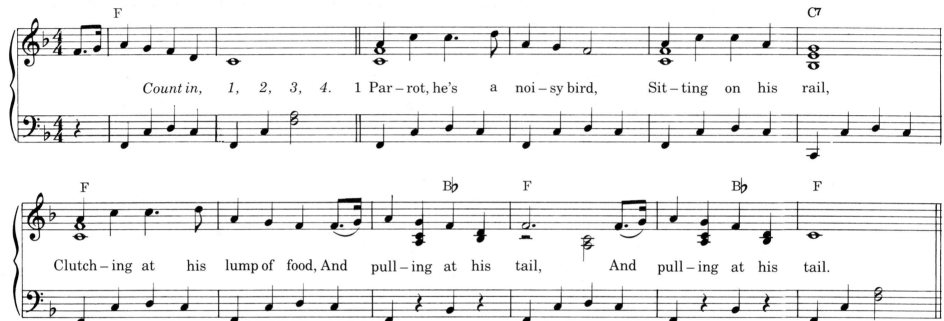

Count in, 1, 2, 3, 4. 1 Par-rot, he's a noi-sy bird, Sit-ting on his rail,

Clutch-ing at his lump of food, And pull-ing at his tail, And pull-ing at his tail.

2 Hamster, he's a cuddly wee thing,
Sleeps the whole day through,
Comes awake when darkness falls,
And seeks out nuts to chew,
 And seeks out nuts to chew.

3 Goldfish cruises round his tank,
Tail flits to and fro,
On and on, he swims all day,
With nowhere else to go,
 With nowhere else to go.

4 Budgie perches hunched and still,
Feathers blue and yellow,
Squawking out his own pet name,
He's a cheeky little fellow,
 He's a cheeky little fellow.

5 Pterodactyl, wild and fierce,
Giant beak and claws,
I don't think he ate today,
 — Children, stay indoors!
 Children, stay indoors!

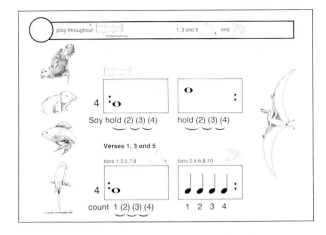

Equipment

Chart 24

Guitar chords: F B♭ and C⁷ (or E A and B⁷ with capo at 1st fret)
Play throughout metallophone (F and high C)
V.1, 3 and 5 triangle (parrot's bell) and woodblock (beak) alternate each bar and should face each other
(Glockenspiel (high C B A G F E D and low C) and (high F E D C B♭ A G and low F)
(Tambour)

To introduce

1 The four-beat note, by clapping it and playing it on metallophone and triangle.

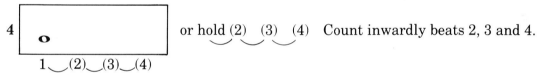

2 The idea of counting and clapping one four-beat note in each bar of **4** time. i.e.

3 The symbol **o** for a four-beat note which could be referred to as an 'egg' – the only note that does not have a stem.
4 The idea of conducting 4 one-beat notes in each bar following this pattern: down/left/right/up.

Follow up games

1 Make up a longer pattern for the class/your friend, i.e. 2 bars in **4** time, or **3** time
2 Teacher made workcard, R.15.
3 Sounds together. (a) One child plays one four-beat note on the triangle, and at the same time another child plays four one-beat notes on the tambour. Repeat the pattern several times. (b) Teacher taps the 'walk' notes with the left hand on the left knee, and at the same time taps the four-beat notes with the right hand on the right knee. Children copy.
4 Playing 8 notes. (a) This time start on high C and come down by step i.e. C' B A G F E D and low C – the C major scale. Teacher then removes all the bars, and asks a child to come out and replace the bars correctly by playing them, to check the sounds. Play descending and ascending scales. Try also the F major scale i.e. high F E D C B♭ A G and F.

69

25 I hear thunder

French tune

Introduction

Count in, 1, 2, 3, 4. 1 I hear thun–der, I hear thun–der, Now don't you?

Now don't you?   Pit-ter pat-ter rain–drops, Pit-ter pat-ter rain–drops, I'm wet through, So are you.

2   I see blue sky, I see blue sky.
Now don't you? Now don't you?
Hurry up the sunshine, hurry up the sunshine,
I'll soon dry, I'll soon dry.

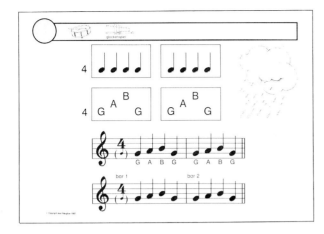

Charts 25–36

Teachers using these charts with older or more experienced children should notice that there is a systematic training in rhythm, along with the introduction of new material. A descant recorder may be used as an alternative instrument for introductions and accompaniments in Charts 25–36.

Equipment

Chart 25 – to be explained one section at a time by covering the chart with a sheet of cardboard with paper clips, which can then be moved down to reveal each section while the teaching points are made.

Drum
Glockenspiel (B A G) with one beater
(Tambourine, xylophone, triangle and descant recorder)

To introduce

1 The idea that on some instruments we can play a tune, while on others, we play a rhythm without a tune.
2 The reading of pitch, i.e. the tune.
3 The stave, i.e. 5 lines and 4 spaces.
4 The G clef or treble clef. This sign tells us that the note G is on the second line of the stave. We use the first seven letters of the alphabet for the names of the notes, so that the note above G is A.
5 The bar, the bar line and the double bar line.
6 The new position for the time signature – this sign tells us that in each bar there are notes and/or rests, which will add up to 4 ♩ beats.

(The key signature of G major is introduced in Stage 2, when the note F♯ is read and played.)

To revise

One-beat notes and a time signature of **4**. ('**4**' is now written as children will see it in published music.)

Follow up game

1 'On which instruments can we play a tune?' Teacher plays on drum, glockenspiel, tambourine, xylophone, triangle and descant recorder.

26 Jingle bells, The fire engine

1. Jingle Bells

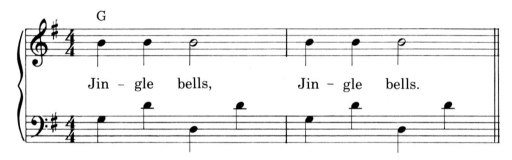

Jin – gle bells,   Jin – gle bells.

2. The Fire Engine

Here's the en – gine on its way!

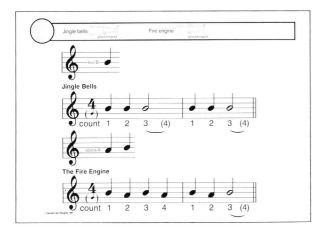

Equipment

Chart 26

Glockenspiel (B and A) with one beater to enable child to play while reading the music
Optional guitar chord: G
(Blackboard)

To introduce

1 The position of B and A on the glockenspiel.
2 The placing of symbols on lines and spaces. These symbols are notes 'on a line', i.e. the line cuts through the notes.

These symbols are notes 'in a space', i.e. the notes are sitting in the space.

3 The symbol for the note B  is on the middle line with the stem up to the right.

The symbol for the note A is in the second bottom space with the stem up to the right.

4 The idea that the notes A to B move *up* by step i.e. from space to line, and that the notes B to A move *down* by step i.e. from line to space. Play these notes.

To revise

1 One-beat and two-beat notes in 4 time.
2 Reading and clapping rhythms. These activities should always precede the reading of the staff names, throughout all the following charts.
3 The singing of the letter names when playing the pitched instruments.

Follow up games

1 'Where are the notes?' On the blackboard, teacher draws notes on the stave and children say whether they are on lines or in spaces. (Ensure that children understand what is meant by 'on the line' and 'in a space'.)
2 Teacher-made workcard, P.1.
3 'Which note is it?' 2 Teacher-made flash cards of B and A for individual note recognition.

27 Song of the Delhi Tongawallah

Hindustani folk song

2 If cruel robbers do way-lay us,
   What to do then? What to do then?

3 Grain and grass be yours in plenty
   If we get home quickly, horse.

Chorus

Chorus

* The Delhi Tonga wallah is a pony-cart driver.

74

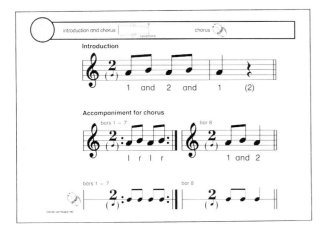

Equipment

Chart 27

Guitar chords: D G and A[7]
Introduction and chorus xylophone (B and A) with 2 rubber/wooden beaters
Chorus coconuts

To introduce

1 The idea of playing the notes B and A for an introduction and then an accompaniment to the chorus.
2 The symbols for half-beat notes (joining bridges) can be written with notes which have either 'heads' or 'feet'.

e.g.

(Children will need to be made aware of how these half beats are written on the stave.)

To revise

1 One-beat and half-beat notes and one beat rests.
2 A time signature for **2** time.
3 Playing with 2 beaters and using alternate hands.
4 Repeat signs.
5 Fast (chorus). Slow (verse).

Follow up games

1 'When do I change?' As in Song 22, stressing the change in pitch from B to A and A to B, Teacher-made workcard, P.2.
2 Class sings the introduction using the capital letters. Then the teacher sings the introduction to 'lah', stopping on one note, and the children say whether it was B or A.
3 Mime playing the instruments with Song 27 on the cassette.

Astronauts

Words by M.B. Wood
French tune

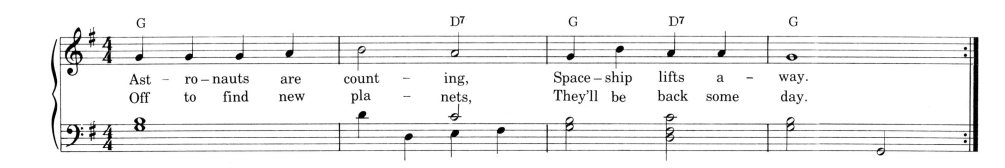

Ast – ro – nauts   are   count – ing,   Space – ship   lifts   a – way.
Off   to   find   new   pla – nets,   They'll   be   back   some   day.

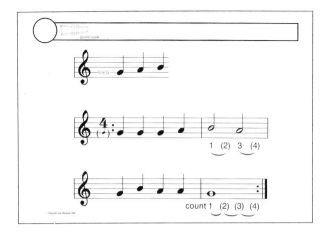

Equipment

Chart 28

Optional guitar chords: G and D^7
Glockenspiel (B A and G) with one beater
(Blackboard)

To introduce

1 The position of G on the glockenspiel.

2 The symbol for the note G is on the second bottom line with the stem up to the right.

3 The symbol for a four-beat note written on a line or in a space

Children could now be made aware of the significance of the G clef i.e. the treble clef, and the fact that the clef sign 'rings' the second bottom line where note G is written.

To revise

1 One-beat, two-beat and four-beat notes.

Follow up games

1 Teacher-made workcards, P.3 and P.4.
2 'Can you write the music for our tune on the blackboard?' (Teacher draws wide stave.) e.g. Bars 1 and 2 of 'Astronauts'.
3 'Which note is it?' 3 Teacher-made flash cards of B, A and G for individual note recognition.

29 Old Macdonald had a band

handwritten top right:
1 Drum
2. Stick
3 Bells

Introduction

Count in, 1, 2. 1 Old Mac-don-ald had a band, 'Ee – I – Ee – I – Oh.' And in that band he

had some chimes, 'Ee – I – Ee – I – Oh.' With a tap-tap here, and a tap – tap there, Here a tap, There a tap, Everywhere a taptap,

D.S. al fine

2 Drums . . . *boom.*

3 Claves . . . *click.*

4 Bells . . . *ting.*

handwritten:
ma-ra-cas = shake.
sticks = Tap.

5 | 14
10
4

1. Instruments. play play
2. Drums
3. Shakers
4. Strips
5. Triangles

Sticks
Drums
Bells,
△'s
shakers

6. Guitars
7. Sandblocks.
8. Bells
9. Gong
10. Instruments

Sandblocks
Drums, Bells. claves

78

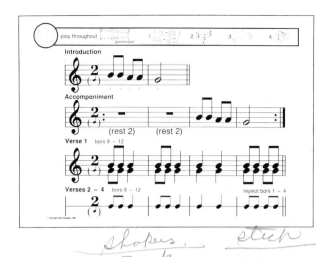

Handwritten notes (left margin): Shakers, Zack, Tobias, Georgina, Becky — etuch Estelle, Alex Tread...

1D
Zackery – Drummer
Georgina ———— v'.
Becky ———— "
Guitar
Andrew Breest.
Andy
Casey
Drew.
Emily
Chimes = Carl

Equipment

Handwritten (top): guitar – chimes Drummer Shakers Sticks, Plunk Ring Boom Share Tap Reece Music Box Tap Reece play → Plunk Boom Toot

Chart 29

Guitar chords: G C and D^7
Introduction and v.1–4; bars 3, 4, 7 and 8 glockenspiel (B A and G) with 2 beaters
Bars 9–12 v.1 2 chime bars (B G) v.2 drum; v. 3 rhythm sticks/claves; v. 4 Indian bells
(Blackboard)

To introduce

1 The symbol for a whole bar's rest ▬ (Teachers will realize that this symbol is used to denote a whole bar's rest in all music in 2, 3 or 4 time.) In **2** time we use the term (rest 2).
2 The idea of playing the notes B A and G for an introduction and accompaniment to the song. If playing the notes B and G together using two children, one reads and plays the note B which has an 'up' stem and the other – the note G which has a 'down' stem.

To revise

1 One-beat, half-beat and two-beat notes.
2 Repeat signs.
3 Conducting 2 beats in a bar. See Song 22.
4 Chord.

Follow up games

1 'Up the steps, down the steps.' Teacher plays B A G or G A B and children tell whether the tune is going up by step or down by step.
2 As a variation, teacher could omit Note A and children tell whether tune has jumped up or down.
3 Sounds together. Teacher plays B and G together on glockenspiel, followed by B and A together. Children say whether they were the same or different, and describe the sounds. Which chord do they prefer?
4 Class sings the introduction using the capital letters. Then the teacher sings the introduction to 'lah', stopping on one note, and the children say whether it was B, A or G.
5 'Can you write the music for the introduction to our song on the blackboard?'
6 Teacher-made workcard, P.5.
7 Conduct 2 beats in a bar with Song 29 on the cassette.

79

30 The clock

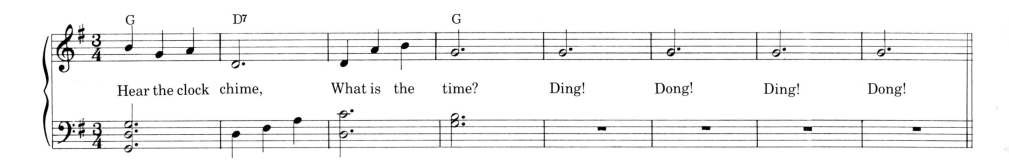

Hear the clock chime, What is the time? Ding! Dong! Ding! Dong!

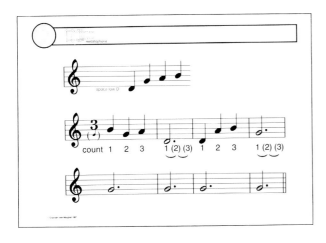

Equipment

Chart 30

Optional guitar chords: G and D^7
Glockenspiel or metallophone (B A G and low D) with one beater
(Tambour)

To introduce

1 The position of low D on the metallophone.

2 The symbol for the note low D ♪ is in the space below the bottom line of

the stave with the stem up to the right.

3 The symbol for a three-beat note written on a line ♩. or ♩.

or in a space ♩. or ♩.

(Teacher should be aware of the positioning of the dot when these notes are on the stave.)

To revise

1 The three-beat note.
2 A time signature for **3** time.

Follow up games

1 'Up or down?' Teacher plays B A G and low D. Children tell whether the sounds go up or down in pitch.
2 Teacher-made workcards, P.6 and P.7.
3 'What is the time?' e.g. After bar 4, teacher or child plays the note G 6 or 8 times.
4 'Can you play these words?' BAG, ADD, DAD, BAD, DAB, GAG?
5 'Which note is it?' 4 Teacher-made flash cards of B, A, G and low D for individual note recognition.
6 Teacher-made musical clock:

(a) Teacher counts in 3 ♩ beats, before the class claps each pattern twice starting at Number 12. Try clapping the patterns clockwise, then anti-clockwise.
(b) 'Which hour is it?', e.g. for two o'clock the teacher taps on the tambour rhythm 12, followed by rhythm 2, while children look and listen.

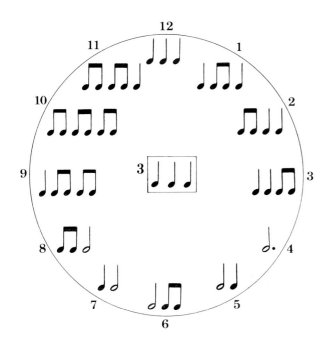

81

Mocking bird

American folk song

Introduction

Count in, 1, 2, 3, 4. 1 Hush lit – tle ba – by, don't say a word, Pa – pa's going to buy you a

mock – ing bird, And if that mock – ing bird won't sing, Pa-pa's going to buy you a *wed – ding ring. 2. And

2   And if that diamond ring is brass,
    Papa's going to buy you a looking glass.
    And if that looking glass gets broke,
    Papa's going to buy you a billy goat.

3   And if that billy goat won't pull,
    Papa's going to buy you a cart and bull.
    And if that cart and bull turn over,
    Papa's going to buy you a dog called Rover.

4   And if that dog called Rover won't bark,
    Papa's going to buy you a horse and cart.
    And if that horse and cart fall down,
    You'll still be the sweetest little baby in town.

or * diamond ring

Equipment

Chart 31

Guitar chords: G and D^7
Introduction glockenspiel (B A G and low D)
Play throughout metallophone (B A G and low D) with 2 beaters
Last verse extra alternative accompaniment to metallophone – 6 chime bars, arranged in 2 groups of 3 (low D F♯ A and G B and high D)
Play throughout maracas or shakers – play very softly

To introduce

1 The idea of playing the notes B A G and low D for an introduction and accompaniment to the song.
2 Chords G and D on chime bars. The G chord uses the chime bars G, B and high D; the D chord uses the chime bars low D, F♯ and A. Follow the guitar chord patterns playing o rhythm, during the last verse. i.e.

G   D   D   G

Follow up games

1 Teacher-made workcards, P.8 and P.9.
2 'When does it change?' Children close eyes while the chime bar players play, e.g. 8 G chords, followed by one D chord. Children respond to the change in sound.
3 Class sings the introduction using the capital letters. Then the teacher sings the introduction to 'lah', stopping on one note, and the children say whether it was B, A, G or low D.
4 Sing the song 'Bingo'. As an alternative activity to the singing game, substitute body sounds, instead of singing the capital letters 'B I N G O', e.g.
   V.1 clap, instead of singing 'O'.
   V.2 tap right knee with right hand for 'G' and then clap, instead of singing 'O'.
   V.3 tap left knee with left hand for 'N', etc.
   V.4 stamp left foot for 'I', etc.
   V.5 snap right hand fingers for 'B', etc.
   As another alternative, substitute five different percussion instruments, instead of body sounds for B I N G O.
5 'Can you write the rhythms for the capital letters B I N G O?'

83

32 Kookaburra

Australian folk song

Introduction

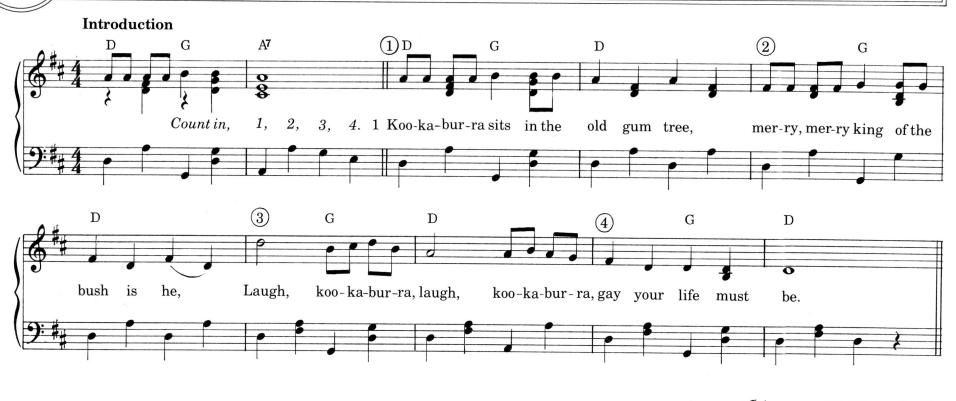

Count in, 1, 2, 3, 4. 1 Koo-ka-bur-ra sits in the old gum tree, mer-ry, mer-ry king of the

bush is he, Laugh, koo-ka-bur-ra, laugh, koo-ka-bur-ra, gay your life must be.

1 Sing in unison with metallophone and guiro accompaniment.
2 Sing as a two- or four-part round, with metallophone and chime bar accompaniment.

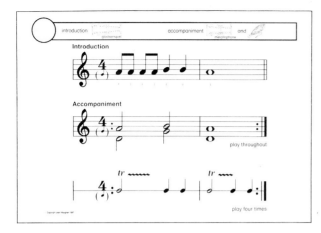

Equipment

Chart 32

Guitar chords: D G and A[7]
Introduction glockenspiel (B A)
Play throughout metallophone (B A G and low D) with 2 beaters for 2 players
Alternative extra accompaniment: 6 chime bars, arranged in 2 groups of 3
(low D F♯ and A and G B and high D)
Guiro – play for unison singing

To introduce

1 The idea of singing a four-part round. As this may prove difficult for some young children it is suggested that the song could be treated as a two-part round, with the second group of children starting after the first group has sung bars 1 and 2.
2 The guiro.

Introductory game

'How many different sounds can you make on the guiro?' Can you play fast/slow, loud/soft sounds?

To revise

1 Playing 2 sounds together (chord), where one child plays the note with an 'up' stem and the second child plays the note with the 'down' stem.
2 Sounds produced by scraping.
3 Chords D and G on chime bars. Follow the guitar pattern, playing

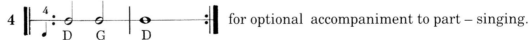 for optional accompaniment to part – singing.

Follow up games

1 Teacher-made workcard, P.10.
2 'When does it change?' Children close eyes, while the chime bar players play e.g. 6 D chords followed by one G chord. Children respond to the change in sound.

Music makers

Swiss tune

Introduction

Count in, 1, 2. 1 We are the mu – sic ma – kers and come from Switz-er – land, We are the mu – sic ma – kers and come from Switz – er – land, We can play the vi – o, vi – o, vi – o – lin, We can play the vi – o – lin and flute. And we can dance___

Chorus

hop – sa la! hop – sa la! hop – sa la! And we can dance___ hop – sa la! Hop – sa la!

86

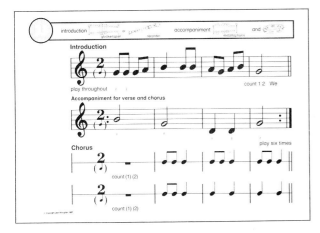

Violin

Big Bass Drum

Slide Trombone

magic flute

Violin = Zuzz

Drun = Boon

Trombone = Doo

Flute = Tweet

2 Clari, clari, clarinet . . .

3 Picco, picco, piccolo . . .

(Actions: Pretend to play the instruments
in lines 3 and 4 of the verses.)

Equipment

Chart 33

Guitar chords: G and D^7
Introduction glockenspiel (B A and G)
Play throughout metallophone (B A G and low D) with 2 beaters
Chorus Brazilian tambourine
(Tambour)
(Orchestral instruments e.g. violin, flute, or records and pictures of them)

To introduce

1 Various orchestral instruments and the method by which they are played.
    The *violin* (a stringed instrument) is held in the left hand, and the bow in the right hand. The bow is then moved across the strings in a downward and upward direction. (Sounds can also be produced by plucking the string with the finger.)
    The *flute* (a woodwind instrument) is like a narrow cylinder and is held to the mouth. The player then blows across a mouthpiece while holding the instrument in a horizontal position.
    The *clarinet* (a woodwind instrument) has a mainly cylindrical shape and is played by blowing into a mouthpiece while holding the instrument in a vertical position.
    The *piccolo* (a woodwind instrument) is half the size of the flute, and is played in the same way, but it's sounds are higher in pitch. (Refer to Song 10 for another example of the link between size of instrument and its pitch.)
2 Making up tunes.

Follow up games

1 'Which instrument do you hear?' After the children have heard and seen e.g. a violin and a flute (or records and pictures of these two instruments), encourage them to discuss the sounds and shapes, and then let them hear one again, for recognition. If any children or adults play these orchestral instruments, invite them to perform to the class.
2 'Can you make up your own tunes?' Teacher-made workcard, C.1, which gives the children rhythm patterns. Children use the notes B A G to make up their own tune and play it. They should say and clap the words, then play the rhythm on one note, before transferring the pattern to three notes. They could be encouraged first to play and sing their tune, then record it either on tape, or with paper and pencil using capital letters. The tune could also be played by a beginner/friend on the descant recorder.
3 Conduct two beats in a bar, as you sing V.3.

34 London's burning

Introduction

Count in, 1, 2. Lon – don's burn – ing, Lon – don's burn – ing, Fetch the en – gine, Fetch the

en – gine, Fire! fire! Fire! fire! Pour on wa – ter, Pour on wa – ter.

1 Sing in unison, with xylophone and non-pitched accompaniment.
2 When the tune is firmly established, sing it in four parts with xylophone accompaniment.

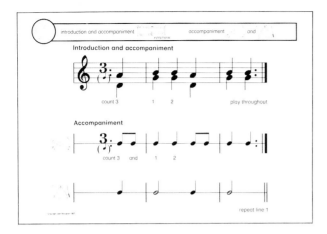

Equipment

Chart 34

Guitar chords: G and D^7
Introduction and accompaniment xylophone (B A G and low D) with 2 beaters for 2 players
Play for unison singing bars 1–4, 7–8 rhythm sticks/claves, bars 5–6 triangle
(Tambour)
(Blackboard)

To introduce

1 The idea that not all accompaniments start on the first beat of the bar. Teachers should be aware that they give a count in of 2 beats, before the players begin on beat 3.
2 Singing and playing a round in **3** time. At this stage, young children may be able to sing a round in 4 parts. Group 2 enters when Group 1 has finished singing 'London's burning, London's burning'.
3 The idea that two-beat notes occur in **3** time.

To revise

1 Conducting 3 beats in a bar, (see also Song 23). (Notice that singers begin on beat 3)

$\nwarrow$3 = London's
$1\downarrow$ $\searrow$2

Follow up games

1 'Can you write the music for our song?', e.g. using the first 2 bars we sing in 'London's Burning' (on the blackboard).
2 Teacher-made workcard, C.2: 'Can you make up your own tune?' As in 33 – using the notes (B G and low D). Give your tune a title, e.g. *Bugle tune.*
3 Play your tune on a recorder.
4 Teacher-made workcard, P.11.
5 Teacher-made domino cards, e.g.

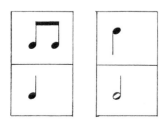  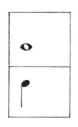 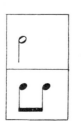 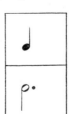 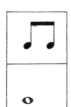 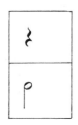 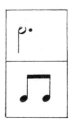 

35 Coulter's candy

Scottish folk song

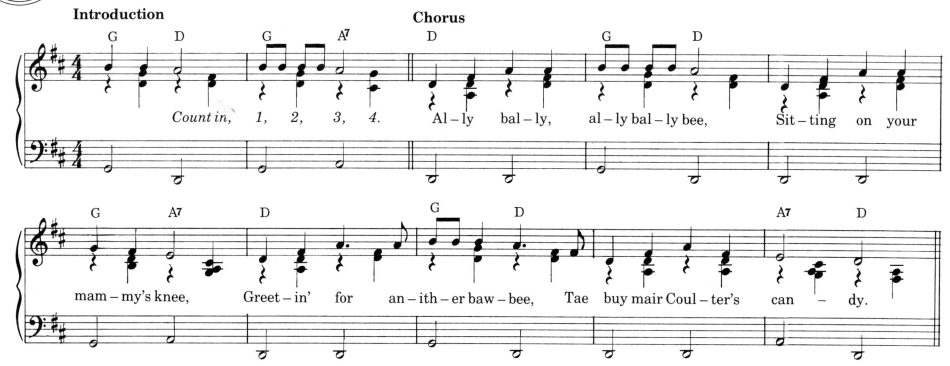

Introduction

Count in, 1, 2, 3, 4.

Chorus

Al – ly bal – ly, al – ly bal – ly bee, Sit – ting on your mam – my's knee, Greet – in' for an – ith – er baw – bee, Tae buy mair Coul – ter's can – dy.

1   Ally bally, ally bally bee,
When you grow up, you'll go to sea,
Makin' pennies for your daddy and me,
Tae buy mair Coulter's candy.   *Chorus*

2   Mammy gie' me a thrifty doon,
Here's auld Coulter comin' roon,
Wi' a basket on his croon,
Selling Coulter's candy.   *Chorus*

3   Poor wee Jeannie's lookin' affa thin,
A rickle o' banes covered ower wi' skin,
Noo she's gettin' a double chin,
Wi' sookin' Coulter's candy.   *Chorus*

Mr Coulter was a travelling candy salesman, who lived in the Borders during the nineteenth century.

Greetin'=crying
anither bawbee=another half-penny
mair=more
gie=give
thrifty doon =money down
roon=round
croon=head
affa=very
banes=bones
Sookin'=sucking

90

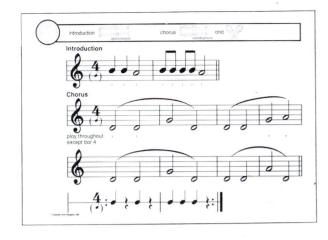

Equipment

Chart 35

Guitar chords: D G and A^7
Introduction glockenspiel (B A)
Chorus metallophone (B A G and low D) with 2 beaters
Chorus maracas or shakers – play very softly
(Tambour)
(Wide-spaced manuscript paper)

To introduce

1 A more difficult and varied accompaniment which reinforces the guitar/piano chords played by the teacher.
(If necessary, one child could play bars 1, 2, 5 and 6 on 2 chime bars low D and G and the other bars 3, 4, 7 and 8 on metallophone.)
2 The phrase. Bars 1 and 2 = Phrase 1. Bars 3 and 4 = Phrase 2.
3 The symbol ⌒ for a phrase mark.

To revise

Conducting 4 beats in a bar. See Song 24.

Follow up games

1 Teacher-made workcard C.3. 'Make up your own tune'. As in 33 – using the notes B A G and low D. Children could write their own tune on the stave, provided the teacher could supply wide-spaced manuscript paper.
2 Teacher-made musical clock:

(a) Teacher counts in 4 ♩ beats, before the class claps each pattern twice, starting at Number 12. Try clapping the patterns clockwise, then anti-clockwise.
(b) 'Which hour is it?', e.g. for two o'clock the teacher taps on the tambour rhythm 12, followed by rhythm 2, while children look and listen.
3 Conduct 4 beats in a bar with Song 35 on the cassette.

36 It's me, O Lord

Negro spiritual

Introduction

Count in, 1, 2, 3. It's me, it's me O Lord, Standing in the need of prayer. It's

me, it's me O Lord, Standing in the need of prayer. 1 Not my brother nor my sister, but it's me O Lord,

Standing in the need of prayer, Not my brother nor my sister, but it's me O Lord, Standing in the need of prayer.

D. S. al Fine

2 Not my mother nor my father, but it's me O Lord,
   Standing in the need of prayer . . . *Chorus*

Sing and play the last chorus, twice, softly then loudly.

Equipment

Chart 36

Guitar chords: G and D^7
Introduction glockenspiel (A G)
Play throughout glockenspiel (B A G) for upper part of accompaniment
Play throughout 2 chime bars (G and low D) for lower part of accompaniment
Tambourine play on the rim throughout

To introduce

1 The idea that three-beat notes occur in **4** time.
2 The term (rest 2 3 4) for a whole bars rest in **4** time.

To revise

1 Playing by ear. The tune of the chorus can be played on 3 notes (B A and G) on the glockenspiel or recorder.
2 Phrases.

Follow up games

1 'Sounds together'
  (a) One half of the class claps the ♩ beat, counting inwardly 1, 2, 3, 4, while the other half sings the tune and at the same time taps its rhythm quietly.
  (b) Repeat this activity, without singing the tune.
  (c) Change over patterns, so that both sections of the class try the other rhythm.
  (d) Class sings and taps the rhythm of the tune and, when the teacher puts up the palm of her hand, the children stop singing and tapping, but inwardly continue hearing the next part of the tune, in their heads. When the teacher drops her hand, the children continue singing and clapping the tune again.
  (e) Repeat this activity, with rhythms only.

  (f) Each child claps the ♩ beat on the left knee with the left hand, and at the same time claps the rhythm of the tune on the right knee with the right hand. Then change over patterns clapping ♩ beat on right knee, etc.
2 How many phrases are there in the pitched percussion accompaniment?
3 'Can you write the introduction for our song?' Remember to put the dot for a three-beat note just above the line. Practise drawing a one-beat rest, before writing one on the stave.
4 Teacher-made workcard, P.12.

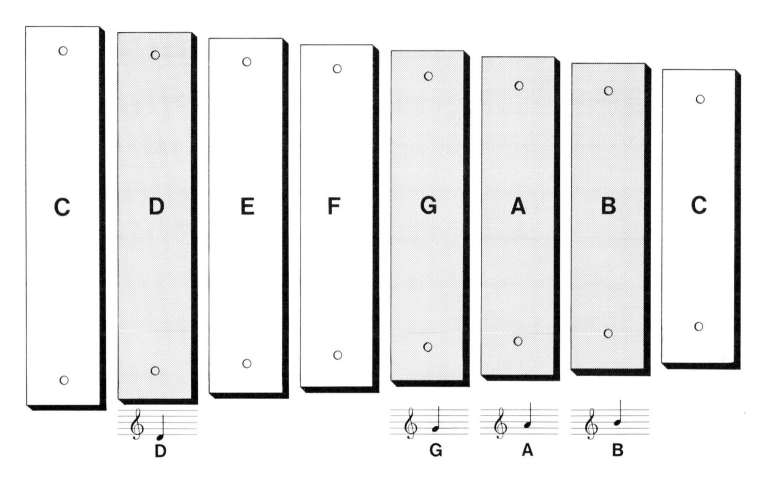

This page may be duplicated and used for practice by pupils without instruments from song 25 onwards.